NATIONAL COUNTIES
BUILDING SOCIETY

National Counties Building Society was established on 3 March 1896 and thus celebrated its Centenary in 1996. At the time of its Centenary the Society had Total Assets in excess of £400 million and served over 30,000 customers. With Reserves in excess of £75 million, the Society had unrivalled financial strength, being amongst the most efficient of all building societies.

The Society was founded by former senior Post Office employees to provide savings accounts and loan facilities for postal workers. In its early years, the Society was based in the City and Strand districts of London but in 1966 it moved its headquarters to Epsom , taking occupation of Waterloo House in the High Street - the town's "finest building" as it is described by John Furniss in his book. By 1991 the Society's growth meant that its operations could no longer be accommodated within Waterloo House and so another of Epsom's historical buildings, Ebbisham House in Church Street, was acquired. The head office staff transferred there but cashiering services remained available at Waterloo House, for personal callers. In 1995 the Society constructed a new branch office adjacent toWaterloo House, fronting onto Ashley Square, part of the Ashley Centre, and cashiering services were relocated, thus ending the Society's 30 year occupation of Waterloo House.

National Counties has successfully developed its business over the last 100 years, attracting customers from all parts of the United Kingdom. It pioneered postal investment accounts, with investors being attracted through national press advertising and offered the convenience of account operation from their homes, using the post. Mortgages were distributed via intermediaries, situated in many parts of the county, but mainly in Southern England. The Society is, however, proud of its Epsom connection and considers itself very much part of the local community. A great many of its customers live and work in Epsom and the surrounding areas and appreciate the convenience of the town centre branch.

The Society is delighted to be involved, during its Centenary Year, with the re-print of this book by John Furniss. Talk of the Town provides an informative and charming insight into the development of Epsom over the centuries. We congratulate the author on his excellent work and express appreciation on behalf of the local community for the sharing of his considerable knowledge of the town.

ONE HUNDRED
100
YEARS
1896-1996

# EPSOM

## *TALK OF THE TOWN*

John Furniss

First published 1992
Second edition 1996

Published by –
John Furniss
Beech Tree Cottage
St. Martin's Avenue
Epsom. KT18 5HS

ISBN 0 9527671 0 4

Printed in Great Britain by The Bath Press, Bath

# *Introduction*

After I retired from business in 1983, I soon found myself being pressed to take on a variety of little jobs. 'Now you've got nothing else to do . . .' was the typical approach.

One of those 'little jobs' I was pleased to take on was to give talks to various local organisations on the subject of Old Epsom and its inhabitants. In time I added the showing of slides as these occasions became more frequent and of longer duration.

By 1988 a number of old friends, who shared my interest in the subject, began to urge me to record my accumulated knowledge in some form – 'before its too late' – as they ominously put it. This is the result of their persuasion.

The book does not, of course, set out to be a comprehensive History of Epsom. Its style, its inclusions and its omissions are undeniably dictated by my own particular interests. It soon became clear that the basic format should be autobiographical.

Having lived, worked and played in Epsom for well over seventy years, and being a member of a family that has been at the very heart of the town for centuries, I hope this will prove to have been the most satisfactory way – through family history and personal experiences – to pass on some knowledge of my native town and its inhabitants to those in the future who may find it interesting.

*John Furniss*
*1992*

# *Chapter One*

Towards the end of 1915 the war was going badly. My father, William George, was imminently expecting to join the Royal Flying Corps, and my mother, Evelyn Jessie, whose first child, 'Baby Billy', had sadly died at six months, was now imminently expecting me. I arrived at No. 11 Worple Road, Epsom, early on Sunday morning, the 12th of December, and my father arrived at No. 11 Squadron, RFC, within a very few months.

Having regard to the fact that both my parents were always known by their second name, it was decided to give me just the one.

In due time it was explained to me that the particular choice had been made because our family had been in Epsom for very many years and the earliest known Furniss in the town was called John.

Much later, when I had the urge to dip into Epsom and family history, I discovered that this particular John Furniss was, in fact, born in Ewell in 1684. The first record of him living in Epsom is dated 1716. He died in 1754 leaving nine children and thereafter seventy-nine traceable great to great, great, great, great, great Epsomian grandchildren, of whom I am one.

No. 11 Worple Road was part of a pair of red brick Victorian cottages next to the little alleyway joining Worple Road to Downside. It still is – though no longer named Ivel Cottage. It still possesses the charming little trellised porch, but not the creamy yellow roses growing round the door.

Not long before my birth the young men of the University and Public School Corps were based in Epsom and billeted out at private houses. My parents looked after two of them at Ivel Cottage, and Mother, not unnaturally, became very fond of them.

My very first memory of my father was seeing him in his 'hospital blue' walking down from the railway station to the shop on the corner of West Street, where the family business of Coal and Corn Merchants was carried on. He was on his way from Horton Hospital, which during both world wars was turned over to military use.

The shop was at the end of that rather unusual building – the first reinforced concrete building in the area, I am informed, – (numbers 26 to 28 West Street) – and had been erected by my grandfather Thomas in the 1870s. It still stands on the corner of what is today called Station Approach, looking rather out of place and defiant against the changing face of the town.

It was in the four little rooms, two up and two down, at the railway bridge end of the West Street building that my Aunty Sis (Sarah) and Lizzie (Elizabeth) lived. They were the children of my grandfather's first wife and born in America in 1853 and 1860 respectively at Yonkers just outside New York. Details of young Thomas' years in America from 1849 and what he found in Epsom upon his return I must recount later.

Of my half-aunts, I particularly remember rooms that seemed very tiny to me, even then, pots of fuchsias, a large blazingly hot 'kitchener' and picture postcards or transfers depicting red coated Boer War soldiers. I remember I was struck by the sadness Aunty Sis showed when she spoke of the plight of the poor little piccaninnies, which I did not quite understand. It does indeed sound surprising, but can be explained in due course. Lizzie was an unfortunate hunchback. Sis was gentle and kind. She taught me the Lord's Prayer and made fantastically hot ginger cake.

I remember barbed wire on the beach at Gorlestone, on the East Coast, and an aeroplane landing on the beach at Boscombe, but do I really remember Kaiser Bill's zeppelins? I think so. At least I have a very clear memory of buying French and Belgian flags on Surbiton Hill to hang alongside our Union Jack. That presumably was in November 1918.

The reason for Surbiton Hill was that my mother took me to live at her father's house, No. 7 Browns Road, Surbiton, during Father's absence. Grandpa Harry Killick was a butcher on Surbiton Hill. He was a keen huntsman – not riding but running with the hounds – a harrier. It is now hard to imagine such activity in Ewell and Worcester Park. It has been assumed that my modest achievements in the athletics sphere between 1933 and 1949 could well have been a legacy from grandfather's years of running, though under somewhat different circumstances. I have been a member of Blackheath Harriers since leaving school and joined Epsom Harriers for a period after the War.

Mother was the second of five daughters – Elsie, Jessie, Trissie, Lilla and Gladys. Elsie and her husband, Jack Anderson, before going to Guildford, lived in Epsom's East Street in the days when the road was little more than half its present width. Their row of little grey houses, now the site of office blocks just beyond 'The Common Room' (formerly 'The Locomotive'), had tiny gardens in front with neat privet hedges, and I well remember a large monkey puzzle tree that particularly impressed me. East Street always seems to have been the most unattractive approach to the town. At the last count there were fourteen office blocks of amazingly varied architecture, but no monkey puzzle trees – in fact hardly a tree of any kind.

My father for many years treasured a postcard sent to him in France during the war from Surbiton, in which I was supposed to have dictated '. . . went to that little pub where the water are'. That was Bones Gate Splash. A modernised version of the Bones Gate pub is still there but, needless to say, vehicles on the Chessington Road no longer splash through a picturesque ford. The combined stream from the Stamford Green and Stew Pond sides of Epsom Common now passes unseen beneath the roadway through an unromantic concrete pipe. The other 'splash' was where the Hogsmill Stream from the Spring in Ewell crossed Ruxley Lane – Ruxley Splash – on its journey to Kingston to join Father Thames. One would hardly guess this today as hundreds of vehicles pour along the wide and increasingly busy road to and from the Kingston by-pass.

The Stew Pond referred to, and its much larger neighbour the Great Pond, have been much improved since the mid 1970s when Ted Dowman, whom I had already met during my activities at NESCOT, and his Epsom Common Association initiated a considerable clean-up and restoration programme over a number of years. These fish ponds were probably created by the monks in the Middle Ages when the land came under the Abbot of Chertsey. 'Stew' has the same derivation as 'steward'. I well recall the muddy swampy Stew Pond as a small boy. Some ten years later it was the scene of my one and only attempt at fishing, when I was taken there by the big boy next door, Ron Harwood – who caught nothing either. Today it is the centrepiece of an excellent nature conservation area.

Harry Killick's father, William, I know only from a photograph, but his sister, Nell Cracknell, I visited a number of times at Cracknell's butchers shop right on the corner by the Spring in Ewell. The Spring refreshed the Roman soldiers when they had their small military camp there close to the Roman Stane Street. The building has been reconstructed recently following a fire, but Ewellians, I believe, still refer to 'Cracknell's Corner'.

The route of ancient Stane Street from London to Chichester is today roughly the straight section of the A24 from North Cheam to the Nonsuch Park entrance, across the by-pass near Ewell Castle School's grounds, the Esso service station, across Langton Avenue, by the Windmill Lane railway bridge, the old Epsom Cottage Hospital, Wyeths Road, near St. Martin's Church, the gardens on the south side of St. Martin's Avenue, across Ashley Road, through The Durdans and RAC parks, crossing the M25 just before coming into the Mole Valley to the north of Burford Bridge.

Aunt Nell appeared to me as a large cylindrical person with enormous hat and veil. The centrepiece of her depressingly dark Victorian upstairs room was a huge purple velvet pin cushion stuck with an amazing variety of hat pins. Her son, Jim Cracknell, ran the butcher's business, which had originally been founded in 1790, and which was finally in the hands of 'Young Jim' Cracknell till the 1970s. It was to this shop that my father in the early years of the century frequently came over on his bike from Epsom to visit Jim's pretty cashier and first cousin, Jessie Killick. They were married on April 6th 1910.

I began by mentioning the Great War, which was to end all wars. People were happily confident of this when official peace celebrations were held all over the land in 1919. In Epsom the celebrations included a great torchlight procession up to the Downs on the evening of July 19th. I can remember being allowed to stay up late that night till about ten p.m. and watching the procession, which included my father and hundreds of others in fancy dress, cross the intersection of Ashley and Worple Roads. I can identify the exact spot in front of Flint House. A programme I have recently discovered shows that, in fact, Father was in charge of the costume arrangements. Prominent Epsom names in the programme as committee members, or in connection with the sports or the refreshments, include Wootton, Langley, Vassar, Trower, Williams and Chuter Ede.

Worple Road in the 1920s was very peaceful, except on Derby Days when it was chock-a-block from early morning till late at night as horse-drawn wagons, carts, buses, carriages and traps constantly entangled themselves amongst the few motor cars in our narrow little road. There was absolutely no traffic control as vehicles and pedestrians just poured up any road leading to the Downs. On their return I particularly recall the happy people, laughing and singing on top of the buses, and throwing some of the aforementioned roses to them from my bedroom window.

On Derby Day Lord Rosebery would sometimes invite King George the Fifth and Queen Mary to lunch at The Durdans before the big race. On one of these occasions as the royal car – a large dark red one – passed the top of Worple Road, I was held up to wave to the King and Queen. I do not recall if they acknowledged me, as did their successors some thirty years later on a certain most surprising occasion. Another Rosebery custom was for the hoi polloi to be allowed to walk through The Durdans' grounds to the races on that one special day in the year. The only Derby I saw in the early days was from my father's shoulders in 1921, when Steve Donoghue, the most famous jockey of his time, achieved the first part of his unique hat trick on Humorist.

I was told that Steve Donoghue, to the cry of 'come on Steve', used to come round Tattenham Corner with his left boot over the rails. I have also heard the same attributed to the greatest jockey of an earlier era – Fred Archer. At the five furlong start I remember once seeing Donoghue at really close quarters – a little monkey of a man with a face like a walnut.

The only other sporting hero of the time I remember hearing of was Jack Hobbs. I had the thrill of seeing him at a charity match at Surbiton, and also once at the Oval the disappointment of witnessing the removal of his middle stump by some fiendish Nottinghamshire fast bowler when he had scored only nine.

Apart from the one memorable annual occasion, Worple Road was very peaceful. To mind comes Mr. Curtis' Ben Hur like milk chariot from which he measured out his gills and pints straight from the churn; my father's black Zenith motor bike, which was kept in that recently renovated little brick coach house with the weather vane on top, between Salcome House and No. 3; and, of course, 'Two Hats'. This often seen character (also known, I understand, as 'Billy Two Hats') was a chopper of wood and feller of trees, and ever since one fell on his head had continually worn two hats, one on top of the other.

One night, not long before my birth, my mother thought she heard a baby crying outside. My father said it was a cat but was persuaded to investigate, and there by the side of the road was a baby wrapped in a blanket. Georgie Worple, as he was at once named, and whom I just remember, lived with a foster mother in Banstead for some years.

I used to pedal my little motor car up and down the alleyway, which still exists today looking much the same, between Ivel Cottage and Downside. For some reason I so vividly remember a fete being held in the field by the side of the pathway and hearing a selection from 'The Gondoliers' being played by a small orchestra. This field is now the site of the Epsom Bowling Club ground.

Another favourite activity was to sail my boat on the pond – then only half its present size – in Rosebery Park, often with John and Jean Roll, the children of Harry and Frank Roll, the builders. My more local playmate, however, lived immediately opposite us. Peggy Liddle's father was valet to no less a personage than the most notable of Epsom's residents – Lord Rosebery. Mr. Liddle, in his formal black suit, was always quietly obsequious, referring constantly to 'his lordship' who did this, or 'his lordship' who said that. A lot more about the 12th Earl will follow.

An annual event I looked forward to was the Fair held at the end of July on the West Street fairground, between the fine old brick wall enclosing Braithwaites' Hookfield House and grounds, and 'The Eclipse' on the West Hill Road. The pleasant grassy space and the attractive wall are still there, but the annual event lapsed after the Second World War. It consisted of the usual roundabouts, coconut shies, chair-a-planes, boxing booths and stalls of various kinds. I particularly remember the roll-a-penny, which could actually produce a profit (but not for long). The fair had its origins in the much older Toy Fair. One can also read of the Shrove Tuesday football in the High Street, but that was many a year before my time.

On the railway by the West Street bridge and the Wheelers Lane turning, and just across the road from the fair-ground, I occasionally used to enjoy watching the steam engines being turned round on the old turntable – a sight denied to schoolboys today. The curved brick wall of the turntable is still much in evidence. It dates from 1859 when the line was still a single track.

Heathcote Road and Worple Road retain some cottages of the old world charm of my early recollections, so let us hope that the people of Epsom and their representatives on the Borough Council will go on resisting the onslaught of the developers in this pleasant part as best they can.

o 0 o

So far as I can recall I rode in a horse drawn cab only once. A few of these cabs used to stand outside Epsom Station in the 1920s, as do taxis today (if you are lucky). My ride was late one night in 1922 on the return from London and 'Peter Pan' – an institution that has managed to survive.

This Epsom station was the second on the site. The first, dating from April 1859, when there were nine trains a day to London, was built when what later became the London & South Western Railway was extended from Wimbledon. Originally this had its terminus at the Leatherhead end of Barnett Wood Lane, before the extension to Dorking in 1867. The present station dates from 1928 when the line was electrified. This process had actually begun in 1925. From then on steam trains quickly disappeared. Eventually the only steam engine to survive in the town was the shunting engine, which visited the Upper High Street goods yard about eleven a.m., to be directed by one Bert the Shunter, who was a wizard at getting the full wagons and the empty ones in their correct positions. This procedure finally came to an end in the 1960s.

Epsom's first station was, in fact, the one in what was then called Station Road – now Upper High Street. Part of it still exists, largely unseen, behind a row of small one-storey shops, and dates from May 1847 when the line, which I first remember as the London Brighton & South Coast Railway, was extended from Croydon. This section was first known as the Epsom & Croydon Railway. The station was called Epsom Town, and was a terminus till 1859. It closed in 1929. I have only just realised that the L.B. & S.C.R. trains (Victoria or London Bridge) for some years passed straight through the L. & S.W.R. Epsom station (Waterloo) on the centre lines where there were no platforms.

The goods yard, which at one time was occupied by all the local coal merchants – Halls, Charringtons, Rickett Smiths, Mogers, the Co-op and Furniss – is today a tightly packed concentration of small houses, as is the one time site of Longhurst's timber yard on the other side of the lines.

Writing of the goods yard in the 1920s and '30s reminds me of something which to young people today must sound quite ridiculous – though amusing. Should the Royal Train be scheduled to pass through, our coalmen were warned to keep the yard tidy, not to be seen working, to stand more or less to attention and, of course, remove their caps. I do not suppose George the Fifth even looked out of the window.

One of the earliest bus journeys I remember was from Epsom to Tooting. This must have been mainly on a No. 70, which from 1924 ran from Dorking to Morden. Originally, I am told, this was No. 107. The 408, which still runs today, began in 1921 as the S6B from The Marquis of Granby in Epsom to Guildford, taking over part of the route of the old 85. The S6B's route was extended to Sutton in 1922 and became the S8. By 1923 it went as far as Croydon and in 1924 was renumbered the 408. By 1939 the 70 had become the 93. The 408 was supplemented by the 470 and both ran from Warlingham to Guildford (or the bus station at Leatherhead). Believe it or not, in the early '50s there were buses along the route every ten minutes. Today's No. 406 from Kingston to Redhill first came into service in 1922 as the S6 – renumbered 406 two years later. It was in 1920 the S6 started from Epsom (Marquis of Granby) to Redhill Market Place. I well remember saving up fourpence in one of my father's tobacco (Old Judge) tins for my first trip to the top of Reigate Hill on a 406. The London General Omnibus Company's red buses for some years had the words 'General' painted on their sides. During the 1930s Henry Pickup ran 'pirate' buses operating on the L.G.O.C.s routes under the same route numbers. I have recently been shown a photograph of one such bus with 'Pickup' on large letters on its side.

o 0 o

From my earliest days I was always aware of the presence in the town of the unfortunate residents of what were then called 'lunatic asylums'; these large and rather forbidding looking places stood a mile or so out in the fields towards Chessington. They were accepted by me as quite naturally part of the Epsom scene.

It was for business reasons very much later – not long before retirement in fact – that I actually saw the interiors of what were by then known as 'mental hospitals'. The Manor, Horton, St. Ebba's, Long Grove and West Park are huge – miles of corridors, enormous halls, large store rooms and kitchens.

It was sometime during the fifteenth century that the Manor of Horton was shed from the lands of the Abbot of Chertsey and became a separate domain. The Act of Parliament of 1845 made the counties and boroughs liable 'to provide asylums for the insane'. Under the Act of 1899 the London County Council, who had just purchased the Manor Horton – some 1040 acres –, assumed responsibility. The Manor, based on the old Manor House of Horton, came first in 1899, then Horton in 1902 and then in 1903, what was originally the Ewell Epileptical Colony, St. Ebba's. Long Grove was completed in 1907. It was to be another seventeen years before West Park was built. To give some idea of the size of these places, Long Grove opened for just over 2400 patients and West Park for just under 2100. The whole complex was the largest anywhere utilised for such a purpose.

In recent years the numbers of patients have decreased considerably and far reaching proposals now exist for the future of the Epsom Hospitals 'Cluster' and Horton Country Park.

During the construction of Long Grove from 1905, the vast amount of material needed was at first transported from the L.B. & S.C. Railway station in Epsom in carts with traction engines. These not only damaged the already inferior roads, but caused a great deal of complaint of noise from the people of the town.

It was then that the standard gauge Horton Estate Light Railway was constructed. The line ran from the L. & S.W.R. station at West Ewell across the lower end of Hook Road, to turn south on to Long Grove. Years later it was extended to reach the new West Park Hospital. It is said that at one time as many as nine hundred workmen per day were carried to the site from Waterloo Station in London and back again. The first engine was nicknamed 'Puffing Billy' and was, of course, a great favourite of the local children. Today some evidence of this little railway, which finally closed in 1950, can be seen in the vicinity of the new Horton Country Club and Golf Course.

o 0 o

My first 'Peter Pan' and first London theatre experience was in 1922. My first experience of wireless was in 1926. This took place at No. 96 High Street. Nos. 94 to 98 still make up the old Yew Tree Cottages, the oldest in the High Street, and according to the detailed researches of Dr. H. L. Lehman is presumably the premises referred to in 1680. More precisely the three cottages were known in time as Percy Lodge, Middle House and Yew Tree Cottage – the yew trees being outside the latter as they still are today. In the days of Epsom Spa, lime and elm trees lined this part of the street. I remember some evidence of this even in my time.

James Bradley Furniss ('Uncle Brad') lived at No. 96. He was the son of one of my grandfather's many brothers, James of G. & J. Furniss, the builders and undertakers. The cottages had been lived in by members of the family certainly since 1801. Uncle Brad had the incredible paraphernalia of batteries, valves, coils and wires spread out all over the green cloth that covered his sitting room table. I so well remember that collection of mysterious technology, but not a thing about the Children's Hour programme from Savoy Hill (2L0 calling).

It was in this house, so I much later learned, that our town's post office was once housed in a single room. The customers remained outside and transacted their business through a hole in the wall.

The Postmaster between 1806 and 1843 was John Lewis Jaquet. During the latter part of this time his landlord was my great great grandfather, Thomas, who was also his tailor and repairer of his clothes. Pownall's 1820 book tells us that the post office was open every night, except Saturday, till eleven o'clock. Jaquet was followed as Epsom's Post Master by William Andrews, who in turn was followed (as Post Mistress) by his widow Lucy, daughter of William Dorling, the printer, till 1891. Their daughter, Mary Ann, held the position till the first year of the present century. There were later post offices further down the High Street and in Waterloo Road, where the library now is, before the building of today's main office in 1897.

The business of G. & J. was run, when I was a boy, by the two sons of James – the younger being Alfred ('Uncle Alf'). When the well-known suffragette, Emily Davison, who threw herself in front of the King's horse, Amner, in the 1913 Derby, was buried in London, it was Brad, in large top hat and regulation funereal trappings, who proudly led the procession in Epsom on what, of course, became a national occasion.

Another regrettable incident, causing a much publicised death in Epsom, occurred when Canadian soldiers were stationed at the military camp at Woodcote Park. Following a drunken riot in June 1919 some soldiers were arrested and put in gaol. During a rescue attempt Station Sergeant Green was killed. This was when the old and rather small police station was, till the early 60's, in Ashley Road, just above Ashley House. The present modern station is in Church Street.

Chadband's, the gentlemens' outfitters, on the southern side of the High Street opposite the Clock Tower, had been established in 1848. James (Jim) Chadband, who had inherited by my time, was a very spruce and dapper man, as befitted his trade. The shop continued in the same line as Mackintosh's and later as Terence Ripley's, and then became Alexander's.

Jim Chadband married Frances (Fan), the daughter of James (of G. & J. Furniss). Brad had married Minnie (Min) Chadband, so our families had a double connection. I used to visit the Chadbands' at Salcome House, a rather dark and gloomy Victorian establishment, both outside and inside, on the corner of Worple Road and Downside. When daughter Olive died, in the 1980s, the house was sold, repaired and redecorated, and now really looks most imposing as a good solid example of the period.

Many people will remember when the large white four storied building, which till recent demolition stood on the corner of Ashley Road and the Parade, was Reid's. That is to say, prior to being Chiesman's and then the Army & Navy Stores.

Fewer will remember when Reid's was in the High Street in the building now occupied by the Nationwide Building Society. I recall Mr. H. L. Reid, dapper in a dark blue suit and wearing gold rimmed 'specs' on a rosy face, as he busily and proudly paraded around his popular shop in the 1920s. What I and all small boys, and I expect girls as well, will remember in particular was that wonderful contrivance of cables and little pots that carried his customers' invoices and payments to the cashier and brought back the receipt and change, whizzing on wires above our heads as the shop assistants pulled little levers to set all in motion. Today's technology may be more efficient but nothing like as entertaining.

When the new Reids appeared in Ashley Road, it boasted a roof garden with a lift and, better still, teas on the roof of what we children thought of as a mini-New York. We were very impressed by a four storey building in our town. There was certainly a good view from the top. The best view in the centre of the town today would be from level 5 of the Ashley Centre car park.

Our family Coal Merchants' business, T. Furniss & Son, replaced one of the horses and carts with a one ton Ford lorry early in the 1920s and, whilst retaining some horses till well into the next decade, had three Fords by 1924. I have a good photo of them lined up outside W. R. Page's garage in the High Street.

It was, however, not Page's but T. Hawkins & Sons who provided these vehicles. Tom Hawkins was part founder of the Epsom Cycle Club as long ago as 1891 and subsequently started his own cycle business in 1896. He was a good cross-country runner and was captain of Epsom Harriers. By 1912 he had the Ford agency, having progressed from bikes to motor bikes, to cars, to lorries and finally (though somewhat later) Hawkins' had a fleet of horse boxes. Tom had four sons following him in the business – Tom, Albert, Fred and Arthur. It is interesting to note that the first three mentioned had as their schoolmaster in Ewell none other than the young James Chuter Ede, who was to become such an important figure later.

There was a highly unusual occurrence in 1929 when old Tom, who was travelling on the 406 bus to Kingston, was nearly killed. The railway bridge by what later became the Rembrandt Cinema (now Cannon), was particularly low and the conductor of the open-topped bus had to go upstairs to shout 'Keep your seats please'. In fact we used to call it the 'keep your seats please' bridge. Unfortunately on one occasion Tom did not keep his seat at the critical moment. It was a most dreadful accident, but he lived till 1940, despite that enormous blow on the head. T. Hawkins & Sons Ltd. remained in business in East Street till about ten years ago.

Page Motors of East Street and the Nonsuch Trading Estate still flourishes today. In the time about which I am now writing, W. R. Page had his garage in the High Street. The site is now occupied by the indoor market by the Post Office. Bill Page bought the premises in 1919. When I was a boy he had, for a short time, a partner in the well-known racing driver Kaye Don, whose Silver Bullet belonged to the same era as the more famous world-beating cars of Seagrave and Campbell.

It was about this time that one of the most noted cars in town was Charlie Langlands' green Bentley – the envy of all small boys (and their dads). Bob Page has recently told me it took forty gallons of petrol at a time, which had to be filled, of course, by winding the handle of the manual pump – a long job. Charlie and Cecil Langlands were well-known Epsom Estate Agents and the sons of Walter Langlands, who also had close connections with Epsom Downs management. C. J. Langlands was clerk of the course from 1926 and chairman of the Epsom Grand Stand Association from 1928.

Bill Page had eight sons and a daughter. Some of his small boys built a little wooden buggy on four wheels, which became one of the sights of the town. They would come crashing down Ashley Road from the top of the downs, sometimes even crossing the High Street by the Spread Eagle, right under the eye of a friendly 'bobby' on point duty, before coming to rest in Waterloo Road.

In 1941 the garage was devoted to war work, and one night a bomb blew a car on to the roof, but nobody was hurt. Son Tom was then in the RAF. He painted the Borough crest on the side of his Hurricane, and it is said that, on one occasion, flew so low over his native town that he bent the weather vane on top of the Clock Tower.

Grandson Richard is the company's present Chairman and is MP for South West Herts. I am indebted to Bob Page for jogging my memory about all this.

Somewhat before my time, where South Street curves round into the High Street, was the Epsom Cycle Works and Epsom Motor Works run by a Mr. T. Hersey. Renamed the Woodcote Motor Company, the garage business moved to Church Street, where I first remember it, on the site now occupied by H. F. Edwards & Co. Ltd. Before Edwards it was the University Motors. A Captain Norman ran Woodcote Motors for some years before George Bulman took it over. It was Bulman's son who for a while had the Farm Garage further up the road. In Norman's days the Manager was a Mr. Swift, who subsequently ran the Ewell Downs Motors at the junction of the Ewell By-Pass and the Reigate Road when the by-pass first opened. I knew his daughter, Hazel, in connection with script writing for amateur theatricals just after the War. Later she had a professional career as a continuity girl in films, and finally became a novelist.

Well-known as fishmongers in Epsom from the year 1838 were Marshalls. A. C. Marshall (Alfred) was one of our Mayors during the Second World War. His brother, Arthur, had been a professional singer on the Music Halls before going into the fish business. During the 1920s and '30s Marshall Bros. had as many as three shops in the town, including the restaurant near the Marquis of Granby. Subsequently Alfred's two sons, Hector and Norris, took over till the last shop closed only a few years ago.

o 0 o

Contemporary with the Yew Tree Cottages and on the opposite side of the road was, and still is, the town's finest building – the Assembly Rooms, known for many years now as Waterloo House, though originally as The New Tavern.

My grandfather would have known this building, one of the most beautiful and prestigious in the area, as Bailey's, the drapers (established in 1770), and my father and I as a small boy as Wheelers. Many of today's Epsomians will still refer to it as Elys. It is currently in the possession of the National Counties Building Society, who I am pleased to know appreciate the history they have inherited.

The large red brick building, raised above the road level at the junction of the High Street and South Street (once New Inn Lane), was built in 1690. It features in various prints, together with the old Watch House and the pond, which was once in the middle of the street. Originally it had a courtyard within it, the open ends not being enclosed till the beginning of this century. It was once one of the largest of such meeting places in any town in the country, and still is in excellent condition. The interior has been much altered, particularly since 1900. The front now has the inevitable out-of-period large plate glass windows. Further restoration was recently mooted but seems to have been precluded so far.

In days gone by it was a busy centre of fashion when it housed meetings, public and private, special social and official events, and saw much drinking and gambling, dances and even theatricals. The large main room ran right across the building at the rear. One can envisage the elegant balls with the crinolines and powdered wigs of the eighteenth century; perhaps also the degrading cock-fighting and bear-baiting which were, unbelievably, considered good sports – and that really not so long ago.

As 'Theatre Epsom' it saw some of the cruder comedy and heavy drama of those days. A poster of 1829 proclaims 'The Proprietor proposes representing the choicest plays by our best authors, whose acknowledged ability added to their regular conduct in their private capacity, he trusts will enable him to the support and patronage of the liberal minded inhabitants.' Nicely put.

In 1742 it housed a revival of Farquhar's well-known comedy, 'The Recruiting Officer', and William Powell of Drury Lane itself is said to have appeared there. He was a protégé of Garrick's and later gained some eminence in the theatrical sphere. No record, however, exists of Thomas Shadwell's 'Epsom Wells' of 1672 being presented there, appropriate as that would have been. The play, in fact judged to be rather a poor one, deals with the bawdy and amorous goings on at our Spa. By all accounts, unlike a certain successor, the Merry Monarch was amused. He asked to see it twice.

When producing or performing at today's Epsom Playhouse, I have often thought of what went on in the magic world of theatre just a few yards away. After all, that ancestor after whom I am named might well, on occasion, have been in the audience. Of course, I like to imagine he might also have been on the stage.

Daniel Defoe, I was delighted to discover, has bequeathed us the following illuminating comments – 'People are particularly apt to make havoc of another's reputation in Epsom', and 'People go to Epsom more for mirth and intriguing than for the physic', and 'Ladies and gentlemen go to Epsom in summer to divert or dabauch or perhaps both'. Quite a place.

o 0 o

Every few years our cellar at Ivel Cottage became flooded. My father explained to me that this was caused by the Bourne or Earthbourne. Those today who have to dig big holes in Epsom for the not infrequent works in Ashley Road or East Street and other places (for instance, the creation of the new Sainsbury's) will know all about the effects of our underground streams and intermittent springs. These are produced by the saturation of water in the chalky downs above, which then permeates through the sand and gravel below at irregular intervals. At one time the underground stream that ran beneath Worple Road would occasionally flood what is now the junction of High Street with East and Church Street.

Before I was very old, I was told our town obtained its name from 'Ebbe's Ham' – that is the home of someone called Ebbe (two syllables), and generally considered to be that of a certain Queen Ebba, wife of a South Saxon King around the end of the sixth and beginning of the seventh century; remembered still in the names of Court Farm, Upper and Lower Court Roads and the Court Recreation Ground. Doubtless Father had this directly or indirectly from the book of Gordon Home (1901) or maybe the earlier one on Epsom by C. J. Swete (1860). We are told these days, however, that it is quite likely Epsom's name derives from the flow and 'ebb' of these subterranian waters. The first explanation is, I must say, the more romantic. Nevertheless, our cellar did keep flooding; and I expect it still does.

The current spelling, first noted in 1607, was preceded over hundreds of years by quite a variety, two or even three of which could have been in use at any one time. These include Ebbesham, Ebesham, Ebsham, Ebisham, Ebbisham and Ebsam.

o 0 o

Certain Epsom shops of my earliest days stand out in the memory – they are mainly connected with food, I may say. Chamberlain's was run by one Bob Chamberlain, the baker, with his plump wife and equally plump sister. As well as a bakery this was one of those lovely old fashioned institutions, now rarely found – a tea shop. It was here, sitting on a hard chair at a little circular table, I sometimes enjoyed a glass of cold milk and a sticky cake called a 'coconut pyramid'. Bob Chamberlain sold the site to Odeon Cinemas and a most attractive and comfortable theatre was opened in 1937. Today it is Sainsbury's.

Almost opposite on what is now part of Marks & Spencer – and for a number of years was the re-built Stevenson & Rush, grocers – was Moseleys. This old fashioned grocer's shop was on a higher level and was approached sideways up a flight of stone steps. William Moseley, who engaged in much personal and rapid chit-chat with his customers, wore the customary uniform of striped apron and straw hat. He kept his commodities in bulk in sacks or bins in the shop, patting up his butter into attractive shapes and weighing out the sugar or the currants into those blue paper bags or cone-shaped holders that have long since vanished from the shopping scene. It was all very friendly and very slow going.

As a child I was always fascinated by the large bottles of coloured liquids in the shop window of Harsant's, the chemists. It is now nearly a century since George Harsant upon seeing my father, then adolescent, pronounced 'Ah George, I see you have some pimples – lose them all when you're twenty.' This really beautiful example of an eighteenth century bow-windowed shop still remains, a jewel in our High Street, but the coloured bottles were removed for safety reasons after the hurricane of a few years ago. I am assured by the present management, however, that most older folk, like myself, tend to refer to the place as 'Harsants'.

Riddingtons was one of the town's oldest and most popular shops for teas and chocolates (I particularly remember those chocolate eclairs). At the beginning of the century it had been Barnards, the pastry cooks and confectioners. Long periods of coffee sipping and idle chatting went on at Riddingtons and there was quite an outcry when it was demolished, after our local Council's unsuccessful tussle with the County Council. As if to add insult to injury in its place appeared the National Westminster Bank, thus substituting one of Epsom's most unattracive buildings in place of one of its most attractive.

Mr. Sheath, the baker just opposite, had a dear little old-world shop. I can still recall the smell of the hot loaves as Len Sheath pulled them from his oven (the same one his grandfather had used back in 1820) on a long wooden peel. Regrettably, another of those 1960-type featureless slabs, first occupied by Norlands, replaced that little building. Equally I remember with pleasure the luscious fat doughnuts with plenty of jam in the middle – coming from the oven of Mr. Carpenter in Ewell Village. He was the father of our present councillor, Bill Carpenter.

C. W. Daniell's paper shop in the narrow eastern end of the street stands out in my memory for one reason. At one of Billy Daniell's parties I was introduced to sticky dates covered in desiccated coconut! Till recently this shop was W. H. Smith's.

It is very noticeable how so many shops in this stretch of the High Street have had a variety of occupants moving in and out over recent years. At one time all seemed so settled.

I have recently been told by someone with a longer or better memory than I, that the sight of rats was by no means uncommon in food shops and eating establishments in Epsom in the earlier decades of the century, though we were doubtless no worse than other towns in that respect.

I have collected a great number of photographs of Epsom – ancient and modern. One of my favourites, which demonstrates how very narrow the High Street was, shows placards outside Daniells with Norman's Stores next door.

George Cockman and John Marshall, of Waterloo Road, have of late produced over a hundred pages of 'Old Views of Epsom Town'.

Dad having been such an old friend of Harry and Frank Roll since they were quite young men, it was inevitable that our families remained close when children arrived. Frank and Lizzie Roll's daughter, Jean, was born just seven days after me. We sometimes shared holidays, or parties, or picnics or tennis. Jean married Bob Seymour, whose sports shop is in Upper High Street.

Frank and Harry with Sam Wiltshire, whose son Cecil is today so closely connected with St. Martin's Church, and others, for some years would walk to Leith Hill and back each Whitsun, and walk to Brighton (back by train) each August. Dad was always an enthusiastic participant.

Old Henry Roll, who I was told tended to end his sentences with a rhetorical 'Don't yer know?', had been a builder at one time with Mr. Taylor – Rolls & Taylor. H. H. and F. Roll Ltd. grew successfully under the shrewd Harry and Frank, building Manor Green Road, Meadway, Ridgeway, West Hill Avenue, Christ Church Mount and, later, Copse Edge Avenue and part of Alexandra Road; later again Hookfield, Eastdean Avenue and Park Lawn Avenue. I well recall Lizzie Roll referring to the price of houses in Hookfield at £600, saying 'However can anyone afford it?'

Roll's built the Ebbisham Hall in Ashley Road and Lloyds Bank in the High Street. Their offices were originally just below the Spread Eagle – 87 High Street, now Michael Everett Estate Office – before moving to Ashley Road on the corner of The Parade. Dad always said Roll's upstairs windows were far too small. Harry would reply, 'You don't go to bed to look out of the window.'

Contemporary were the well-known timber merchants, Longhursts. Harold had two sons, Harrison and Stanley. The latter served for some time on the Forestry Commission. Sadly neither had children to carry on their considerable business. Harry and Bessie Roll's son John, my good friend, sadly was killed in Normandy in 1944, shortly after D-day.

One could not omit from the pleasant memories of Epsom in the 1920s a dear little lady named Polly Wyeth. Throughout the decade, and maybe it was well into the 1930s, she retained her Edwardian dress, and never seemed to grow any older. I can see her now in pale lavender, complete with large hat, veil, long gloves and, of course, a parasol. Was she just a pretty lavendar grey ghost parading up and down the High Street of my boyhood? Apparently not, for I have met a number of contemporaries who share the same nostalgic and happy memory. Wyeth's Stores once occupied the corner site between West Street and the top of the High Street.

A less happy memory is of buying new shoes. These always had to be black, stiff and too tight. They would come from a shop called Beams (later Elliotts). That was before Mr. Freeman, Mr. Hardy, Mr. Willis, Mr. Clarke, Mr. Lord and Mr. Dolcis invaded every town in the country. George Beams was at one time Chairman of the Epsom Urban District Council, and he adopted the slogan, 'Why should Epsom wait?' Each burgess in the town today will doubtless have a list of those facilities for which they think Epsom should still not have to wait.

The front cover of the Epsom Horticultural Society's 1914 programme consists of sixteen amusing caricatures of well-known Epsomians of the time. I supplied notes on these gentlemen a few years ago for the Bourne Hall Museum, and of seven (Lord Rosebery, Rev. E. W. Northey, Col. Houlder, Frank Wootton, Walter Langlands, George Duller and George Furniss) will have more to write in due course. I might, therefore, give a few notes on the remaining nine here: Doctor Daniels of Coulthurst, St. Martin's Avenue, and his Hillman – a popular car with doctors at the time; Sir Thomas Bicknell of Hylands House, Dorking Road, a High Court Judge and founder of the Epsom Rifle Club in 1899. Then 'Appy Jack, who lived rough on Epsom Common – frequently drunk – it is said the magistrates repeatedly paid the fine themselves. According to my father he finally told the Chairman of the Bench, 'I'll never do it agin, guv'ner. I'll leave the country. I'll go right down t'other side o' Dorking!' 'Bobby' Capon – Captain of the Fire Brigade and Engineer & Surveyor of the EUDC – wearing the pith helmet that appeared each summer. Basil Braithwaite of Hookfield House – bought by his father Isaac in 1868 on the highest point of Clayhill. For some years following the Second World War the house became the Hookfield Hotel run by the Burnham Brothers. Basil's daughter became the celebrated actress Dame Lilian Braithwaite, so outstanding in comedy. The Tout – a horse racing tipster – who wrote regularly for a number of London journals. The Rev. Bainbridge-Bell, Vicar of St. Martin's, and probably the first person in Epsom to ride a motor cycle – a 3¾ hp Douglas. The Rev. Henry Bowles – the very tall Vicar of Christ Church on Epsom Common. Jack Brewer – one time keeper of the stables behind the Queen's Head in South Street, before operating the town's first car hire business. His daughter is believed to have been Epsom's first lady driver.

Not included in the programme and belonging to a slightly earlier period, I must mention Robert (Bobby) Dearle, the wax and tallow chandler and melter, who for 67 years occupied the same High Street site – now part of Sainsbury's. He was supposed to have been present at seventy seven Derbys. When Ladas won Lord Rosebery gave him fifty pounds and a ride in his coach.

Tom Miles, the greengrocer on the current Barclays Bank site, had the popular shop that remained in the same family for generations. I remember Charlie in my time. According to an old cutting I have, Tom would sometimes sell giant rhubarb leaves as sunshades for racegoers. The only member of the family I knew was Maurice, and in a quite different connection. He was for a time the conductor of the Ulster Symphony Orchestra.

On the subject of greengrocers – post-war characters of note must include the colourful Poultons, vocally notable both in the High Street and the Market, and also little 'Guv' Wates, of No. 102, next door to our shop, with that cigarette that dangled from his mouth whether he was selling oranges or cooking beetroots in an old bath in the yard.

One of my father's favourites when young was Cranky Barnard, who, wearing a dressing gown inside out, would cast stones at the Clock Tower whilst reciting passages from the Bible. He was a harmless old gentleman nevertheless.

An old Epsomian has informed me recently that Cranky Barnard lived at the corner of Ashley Road and the High Street. He had a small plot of grass where there is now a space by the Next shop – that is to say, between what was once the White Hart and Longley and Broadhead's, the Estate Agents and Surveyors. It appears that each spring he turned his grass upside down, with the result that it became considered the best grass in Epsom – not so 'cranky' perhaps?

I formed the impression that everybody in Epsom knew everybody else. In the town today I may recognise nobody at all, or on a very good day get 'hello John' from perhaps half-a-dozen. My father would have a 'hello George' from most of all the twenty people there were between West Street and Lloyds Bank. I expect it was 'hello Tom' from everyone in grandfather's time. Upon his arrival in the town, Lord Rosebery commented upon the 'little sleepy town' he had come to live in. Charles Dickens said the town was so quiet that 'a cannon ball might be fired from one end of Epsom to the other without endangering human life'. My namesake of the early eighteenth century certainly called it 'the village'.

Despite the newer houses, a few undeniably ugly ones and what now seems to be called 'in fill', the Worple Road area, where we lived and in which I still live, has not changed too much or too badly. Downside is still recognisable, and St. Martin's Avenue retains at least some of its Victorian and Edwardian houses, though the road has long since ceased to be of pot-holed gravel.

Rosebery Park, donated to our town by 'His Lordship' in 1913, is still there for our pleasure. Today this possesses far more interesting trees and bushes, as well as the addition of flower beds. Unfortunately it also possesses the addition of vandals who do their best (or worst) to destroy them. Young trees, donated by the Epsom Protection Society and planted by the Mayor, Norma Fryer, at a little ceremony I attended just a few years ago, did not last long. Lager cans, plastic cups and fast food wrappings are, however, not so much in evidence as a year or so ago.

# *Chapter Two*

During the time we lived in Worple Road, my brother Robert (Bob) was born in 1920. I remember being banished for the day to the Wallace's in Church Road, where I played with Betty Wallace and Tony Pickering, and for the first time heard a gramophone. This belonged to Tony's father next door and played cylindrical discs. Ted Wallace and Wilfred Pickering were old family friends and were both senior officers in the Epsom Rural District Council. Their offices were at Ashley House. The rural council ceased to exist in 1933 when the Epsom Urban District Council took over the parishes of Ewell and Cuddington. Banstead then had its own council, till much later becoming part of the Borough of Reigate and Banstead. The Clerk of the E.R.D.C. was Arthur Cotton, a well-known local solicitor. Wilfred Pickering went on to become the Planning Officer of the Surrey County Council.

It was with Betty Wallace that I remember picnics and playing in the hayfield on Mount Hill in South Street. This is now nicely laid out as public gardens (Mount Hill Gardens), leading from the road very sharply up to Rosebank, and with a pleasant view across Rosebery Park. Once upon a time my grandfather was allowed to use this hill for turning out his cart horses in summer and for hay making. The coalmen, I am told, were well supplied with barrels of beer. Uncle Tom and my father carried on this practice into the 1920s. On the town side was Mount Hill House, the home of Colonel Houlder. It is currently the Surrey County Council's Trading Standards office.

I remember most vividly going into the Cottage Hospital in Alexandra Road in October 1922 to have my tonsils out.

This hospital was built by public subscription in 1887, celebrating the Golden Jubilee of the reign of Queen Victoria. It replaced the very small original Cottage Hospital, of fourteen years earlier, in Pikes Hill. It was always so well thought of that people were sorry to lose it and its well respected Matron, Freda Allen M.B.E., just a few years ago. The latest Epsom and Ewell Community Hospital was opened by the Duke of Kent in the grounds of West Park in November 1990.

The very next day after my operation, when I was only seven, believe it or not, for lunch they provided me with a large plateful of cold salt beef.

When I was in hospital many of my little friends from Miss Shaw's school sent me post cards, some of which I still have. Isabel Shaw's school was then just a one room building at the top of Park Hill Road, Ewell, about twenty feet square, and really little more than a shed. My first teacher was a very popular Miss Giles, whom I imagined to be quite old though she was probably about twenty. The little schoolroom is still there – some sort of store. In time Miss Shaw's, with enlarged buildings, it became Park Hill School. For many years now, incorporating Lynton House in the Epsom Road, it has been part of the successful Lynton Preparatory School, whose Principal, Mrs. Vera Thorns, was, when I first knew her as a teenager, a successor of my Miss Giles.

In Epsom at about the same time was a school known as Miss Gray's, at the Lecture Hall in Station Road. It is, I know, still remembered by certain elderly Epsomians.

Miss Shaw's brother was 'Charlie' Shaw. We called him 'Whiskers', and were always impressed by that flask of whiskey that kept coming out of his waistcoat pocket. He became Mayor of Epsom and Ewell in 1937 and in 1940, having been at one time Chairman of the Water Works Committee and much involved in the creation of the Swimming Baths and Baths Hall in East Street opened in 1939 – now christened the Rainbow Centre. It is interesting to note that the original was dubbed a 'white elephant' at the time.

Amongst the pupils of our much loved Miss Giles was Marjorie Longhurst. The Longhurst's were undertakers in both Epsom and Ewell. It was Len Longhurst of Epsom who eventually took over the undertakers part of the G. & J. Furniss business. Another pupil was Maudie Duller of the well-known family of race-horse trainers. George Duller was also a great motor cyclist.

The family business of T. Furniss & Son, Coal and Corn Merchants, was run by my Uncle Tom and my father, the younger brother – the latter being manager of the corn department. It was by accompanying him occasionally on his visits to the stables of Dullers, Nightingalls, Woottons and Hyams, to sell hay, straw, oats and so on that I learned something of the racing fraternity of that era.

Other pupils at Miss Shaw's included Jean and John Roll and the six Youngs, whose father, Tommy Young, was the manager of the Water Works in East Street. The boys were particularly naughty; the girls were petite and blonde, I well remember. There was also the attractive Avis Lane, who wore an emerald green sweater. Emerald green became my favourite colour.

We used to catch the bus from Park Hill Road to Epsom High Street every day, paying a penny to 'the monkey man' – that's what our regular conductor looked like, so we thought.

o 0 o

When in 1923 it was decided that Ivel Cottage was too small for the growing family (and it was thought, so I am told, the pasty-faced elder son might benefit from the open space and higher altitude) we moved to the Reigate Road, Ewell. 'Three Firs' was the middle of the only three houses above Longdown Lane. E. G. Harwood, whose sons Ronald and John still live in Epsom, was the builder and our near neighbour.

The Reigate Road was then a quiet country road with various horse-drawn vehicles, as well as a few motor cars or motor bikes and sidecars, passing rather slowly along. Longdown Lane was rough and hedge-lined, with a couple of small farm cottages at the Reigate Road end and just John Wallace's farm house by Epsom College at the other.

Our telephone number was easy to remember – Epsom 777. I did not, till very many years later, realise that Epsom in 1912 had the first automatic (dial) telephone exchange in the country. In time Ewell had its own exchange and we became Ewell 1777.

Mr. Harwood, previously of Worcester Park, had built three houses in the Reigate Road by 1923. He subsequently continued up and down the road, building all of Ewell Downs Road, The Green and Higher Green during the 20s and 30s. 'Old' Mr. Harwood was a clever man. He invented an enormous wireless set which covered, in amazing bits and pieces, much of one room in a not too large house. He claimed he could, on favourable occasions, tune in to America and other far parts of the globe.

My brother, Bob, and I living in what became No. 116 naturally became close pals with the two boys at No. 114 – Ron and John Harwood. To our delight what still remained of their father's old 1904 Peugeot car, tyreless and abandoned, was made to work in fits and starts up and down their garden. The engine though not the rest of it is, I am told, still in existence. We also spent hours digging holes, trenches and even tunnels in the chalk that was only just beneath the surface, living well on the way up to the Downs, where, of course, there is practically no depth of soil at all. Mr. Harwood had also provided a swimming pool. This was not the modern conception. It consisted simply of a large concrete tank about 15 by 6 feet filled by a hose from the kitchen tap and frequently littered with old leaves and rotten apples.

In later years Ron and John took over the expanding business and created a considerable estate in Woodcote on land acquired from General Northey; building Woodcote Hurst, Chantry Hurst, Sunny Bank, Hambledon Hill and Vale, Cedar Hill, Oak Hill and Pine Hill. Ron has, I know, continued to play a valuable role in the town, in Rotary and on the committees of various organisations. I am most grateful to him for his interest and assistance in my reminiscences, and great help in the publishing of this book.

Playing with our Great Dane dog also featured largely in our daily lives. 'Despard' (from 'Sir Despard Murgatroyd' in 'Ruddigore') was considered by the Rank kennels in Leatherhead, where he came from, to be the largest of the breed they had ever seen. Sadly he lived but five years. James Rank was the miller, who became famous as the head of the great entertainments empire.

Our garden, which today has three houses upon it, was of one acre. During the General Strike of 1926, when Furniss' coalmen were, of course, brought to a standstill, Father and the men took the opportunity to make a tennis court. This was known as 'Cook's Court' after the Union leader, who played a large part in the dispute.

The move from Epsom to Ewell meant a long walk home from Miss Shaw's school. The route commenced along the main road to Half Mile Bush. This was the traditional boundary point between Epsom and Ewell, although a lot more than half a mile from either. There has been no actual 'bush' for many a year. The site is now the less romantic but more useful Texaco service station. I then turned up Windmill Lane to Windmill End and into John Wallace's fields, where the present road still keeps the farmer's name, and then by the little house where Tom Walls lived before moving to the grander 'North Looe', almost opposite 'Three Firs'. Finally my trek was through the cornfields to Longdown Lane and so home.

Tom Walls was the famous comedy actor and partner of Ralph Lynn in the highly successful series of Aldwych farces of the 20s and 30s. Ralph Lynn lived in Hylands Road and subsequently Wilmerhatch Lane. Their successes included 'Tons of Money', 'It Pays to Advertise', 'A Cuckoo in the Nest', 'Rookery Nook', 'Plunder' and 'Thark'.

Fired with enthusiasm from my father's local theatrical activities (I had seen him by 1923 in 'Merrie England', 'The Gondoliers', 'Ruddigore' and 'The Yeomen of the Guard' at Leatherhead, as well as his productions of 'The Pirates of Penzance' and 'The Mikado' at Kingston), I had the urge, even then, to produce my tiny colleagues in some kind of 'show' – a musical of course – but that had to wait a few more years. Twenty-six in fact.

At the age of eight, it was time for me to leave Miss Shaw's and go to a 'prep' school. This was duly arranged, but as the time approached, in the summer of 1924, my parents were to learn that all was not well. It appeared that some of the parents of pupils at my intended school had raised objections to the son of a local tradesman being admitted. Father was not too surprised and, of course, it bothered me not at all. In September I went off to Dower House School in Wallington, wearing a smart blue cap – actually nicer than the rather bright green one from which I was debarred.

Gilbert's Peers had but recently sung 'Bow, bow ye Lower Middle Classes'. Now at the very time we were being reminded of the gulf between profession and trade, my mother was enjoying the services of a maid, the daughter of a Smallholder further up the Reigate Road, who attended her at the ring of a little handbell, wearing the appropriate uniforms for morning and afternoon. The L.M.C's had their own social tiers. If any of our grandchildren ever get around to reading this, will they be horrified or amused?

o 0 o

Dower House School was run by a Mr. and Mrs. Lycett. The whole place was Victorian – one felt almost Dickensian – with no electricity, yellow flickering gaslight, Eton collars and, what was even worse, Latin. Much in evidence was a large map of the world with those parts on which the sun never set coloured bright pink. One day in 1929 when I was, I suppose, particularly dull, 'Lybo' – who could be very sarcastic – announced to the rest of the school: 'I think Furniss is in mourning for Lord Rosebery.' His Lordship had died the previous day. Another of his remarks I remember was, 'We don't want any of your Epsom cunning here.' The word 'Epsom', by the way, produced giggles from the boys, who seemed to associate the place not with salts but asylums.

I was what was termed a 'weekly boarder'. Mrs. Lycett's pièce de résistance was the cutting of a herring into three at breakfast time. One boy got the head, one the tail, and the lucky one got the middle. The boarders told incredible stories in the 'dorm'. 'Dorm feasts' were sometimes held on Mondays if the weekly boarders had smuggled in enough food. I don't know how many gooseberries, plums, and even sardines got hidden in the ventilators. The maid, Violet, served a dual purpose. She secretly sneaked up pieces of cold pudding at night and also gave us pieces of information about the facts of life. The former were the most useful at the time.

The journey to Wallington on Monday mornings was usually undertaken with my father in his Trojan. This was an open car, rather like a tin bath, that had to be started up by pulling a lever, and ran on solid tyres. Trojans were actually made at Croydon. By 1928 they had 'balloon' tyres. The Friday afternoon return journey necessitated a tram to Sutton and bus to Ewell. Later the 164 bus came into operation and, for a short period, ran down the Reigate Road, Ewell, on its way from Banstead to its terminus at Epsom Station, thereby depositing me right outside 'Three Firs'. Subsequently it went over the Chalkpit hill and down College and Alexandra Roads.

It was in the hot summer of 1928 that Bob and I, together with a lot of other people, got paratyphoid B. Our family doctor was Dr. Braidwood, who lived in a large house which still stands, though recently somewhat disfigured, in Burgh Heath Road. Upon his arrival one afternoon, he immediately sat on my bed, right on top of one of my feet, and, without even inquiring into the state of my health, took 'Gulliver's Travels', which I was reading, out of my hands and began to read it himself. About twenty minutes passed as my foot became more and more numb. Suddenly he slammed the book shut and with the single word 'Rubbish' swept out of the door.

Going to a 'prep' school meant smart school clothes and it was Arthur Bowden, who had been in business since 1898 (originally as a 'Breeches Maker'), who provided them – grey suit, black tie and Eton collar. Mr. Bowden had, since early in the century, leased a shop in Station Road (now called Upper High Street) from J. Sainsbury's. He continued till the end of the 1920s when the old Epsom Town Station closed.

This rather pleasant parade of Edwardian shops – known importantly as 'Grand Parade' – still exists, though not easily appreciated in today's traffic. It included Epsom's first Sainsbury's – in two separate shops.

On the opposite side of the road was once the Epsom Collegiate School, run by an elderly Mr. Hillman, next to Norringtons. The old Congregational Church Lecture Hall, further down, was unused and partly hidden by shops, its entrance a home for old tin cans and waste paper for some time during the 1980s. Recently it was badly damaged by fire and had to be demolished in 1991. The Congregational Church (now United Reform) is in Church Street. For many years its Minister was the Rev. E. J. Hitchcock, who was also Principal of the Doctor Barnardo's Home in East Street, where Clayton House is now. He was the father of Lowell, Howard and Edith, all closely associated with local theatricals. In more recent years at the United Reform Church I knew and enjoyed listening to the eloquent and amusing Rev. D. Ellis-Lewis. The Baptist Church is also in Church Street.

Arthur Bowden, plump and shiny faced, with a tape measure round his neck, looked so like Winston Churchill that on one occasion during the Second World War he was officially asked to act as his double. For what purpose I know not. Top secret. Some thought he looked more like Mr. Pickwick. In 1929 his son Lester started the highly successful business that flourishes today at 109 High Street, run by his sons Warwick and Richard.

Part of their extensive business has been the supplying of racing colours to many notable owners. Lester once received a telephone call and the voice at the other end announced he was speaking from Buckingham Palace. The voice was promptly told by Lester, who could be somewhat forthright, to buzz off – or words to that effect – assuming that one of his boys was playing a joke on him. It was not a leg-pull, however, and before long Bowden's found themselves with a much valued customer in the person of the Prince of Wales.

Our family has had a close association with the Pullingers throughout the present century. E. G. Pullinger was at one time the Registrar. He signed my birth certificate.

In my early days, Pullingers, Booksellers and Stationers, was on the corner of the High Street and Waterloo Road – a site that today would be in the middle of the road in front of Lloyd's Bank. Earlier this was Andrews, whose printing office dated back to 1821. Norringtons, the butchers, were next door. James

Andrews' book, 'Reminiscences of Epsom', dated 1904, has recently been reprinted.

E.G's son, Frank, I first remember as the 'Pirate King' with the Leatherhead Operatic Society at the Victoria Hall as long ago as 1926. Subsequently I came to know him well in the Epsom Operatic Society and through our businesses. Frank was a much respected Epsomian one relied upon for kindness and advice. His more mercurial younger brother, Philip (Phil), when about fourteen, came with the rest of the family, which included sister Madge, to 'Three Firs' to look after the house and 'Despard' whilst we were on holiday in 1924. From that time I have seen much of Phil, who never ceases to remind me, some fifty eight years on, how he played 'Simon Slinks' in 'Miss Hook of Holland' when I was just old enough to be in the chorus. Madge married Richard Fentiman, who was once the conductor of the Epsom Choral Society. Like her brothers, Madge was also a singer. Richard Fentiman (junior) I see frequently at the Epsom Playhouse, where he is on the staff. It is Frank's son, Nick Pullinger, who now controls the family business.

Just before the eastern part of the High Street was widened in the 1930s, Pullinger's moved a little further down the street, swapping positions with Lloyds Bank. Their recent shop was consequently just to the rear of that. Lloyds demolished the old Andrews/Pullinger's building and had erected a larger bank in its place by 1935. Almost immediately the Surrey County Council changed minds and authorised the widening of the road. Lloyds began building what is their present bank to the rear. Roll's were the builders. The intermediate building was occupied only for a very short period so, needless to say, the whole affair caused much comment and for a time provided our local newspapers – the Herald and the Advertiser – with plenty of critical material. The High Street programme was finally completed in 1938.

Epsom's first bank had been Mangles Bank, almost a century earlier. We then had the English Joint Stock Bank and that was on part of the site of today's Sainsbury's.

The demolition of one side of the narrow end of the High Street saw the end of three places I well remember – Mills, the photographers, in a little precinct with grass and some bushes, with Skiltons, the butchers, almost adjoining; and the tall Railway Inn three doors further down, which was replaced by the new Charter Inn. As for the other side of the road – the southern – that remained looking thoroughly old fashioned for a long time, and is even now only being rebuilt in parts.

Approximately on the site of the new Curry's and Robert Dyas was once Busbridge's wines and spirits shop. The Busbridge family also, at one time or another, ran The Rising Sun in Heathcote Road, The Wellington in the High Street and the Downs Hotel. It was many years ago that Alfred and Hannah Busbridge, of old Epsom families, lived in the Chase Road area, and it is said it was Hannah who lent old Henry Roll the money to build the original houses in Chase Road, where I first remember the families of Harry and Frank living.

It was Alfred's and Hannah's younger son who had The Wellington. The elder, Harry, was an architect employed by Henry Andrews. Daughter Eleanor was the mother of Douglas Heywood, now living in Woodcote, for twelve years Chief Quantity Surveyor to the S.C.C. Architects Department, who recently gave me this further Epsom family information.

On a certain occasion when Lord Rosebery was just coming out of St. Martin's Church (before the time he transferred his attendances to Christ Church), smoke was seen rising in the area of The Durdans. Alfred Busbridge, as Captain of the local Volunteer Fire Brigade, took charge. Whether Alfred took ample supplies from his wines and spirits shop, or whether His Lordship was over generous I do not know, but by all accounts the members of the Brigade became blind drunk and could not return to base till many hours after the fire had been finally extinguished.

The horse trough that stood for so long at the junction of the High Street with East Street, Station Road and Church Street, is now preserved outside the Rubbing House on the Downs.

I have already made mention of Curtis, Rolls, Reids, Hawkins, Pages, Bowdens, Marshalls, Langlands, Beams, Miles, Harsants, Moseleys, Longhursts, Pullingers, Chamberlains, Daniells, Riddingtons, Sheaths and Busbridges. Others I remember from my between-the-wars years include:

Nelsons – The Epsom Riding Establishment on West Hill. Nelson's pool will be remembered with pleasure.
G. Skelton & Sons – Builders of 67 South Street.
H. F. Trower – later Scraggs – Forage and Seed Merchants in South Street.
Randall & Measures – For Table Waters and their speciality – Home- brewed Ginger Beer.
Measures & Randall – Car Hire.
Cropley Bros. Ltd. – Len Cropley was a likeable and very cheerful character; builders office by The Albion; works in Church Road.
Mortimers – Chemists on the South Street corner.
Ardern Elphick – Butcher. Next to the Marquis of Granby. Formerly Bradnams. Doris Elphick was notable in local drama.
Freddie Roast – A popular Epsom character – with his wonderful selection of household items.
Holland & Barrett – Grocers. I recall their regular deliveries.
Snashalls (George Snashall) – from China and Glass to Toys and from Brooms and Brushes to Cricket Bats; by The Wellington.
Dorset & Co. – Ironmongers. By Snashalls; originally on the Waterloo Road corner till 1906.
Cragg & Lewis – 113 High Street – 'Everything for Baby'.

Weston & Co. – Music Shop. Gramophones from £4. 15. 0. '78' records at 4/-d and 2/6d.
Tottles – the Chemists.
Archie Hicks – Haircuts 6d (4d for Father who was bald).
W. J. Keeling – Furnishing. Old building recently replaced for Robert Dyas and Curry's.
Andersons – Jewellers. Mark Anderson currently at what is known as Nell Gwynne House.
Nuthall & Co. – Grocers. Betty Nuthall was a Wimbledon tennis champion.
C. J. Roe – Chemists of 6 High Street.
J. Woods & Sons – Bakers of 10 East Street.
F. Williams (Fred) – Hairdressers of 7 Station Road.
Herbert Watson – Florist, 19 Station Road.
Riddick, Charles – Jeweller and watchmaker.
Absolom & Garland – Ironmongers. Hilda Absolom married Ralph Furniss. Their son was Brian.

To revert to Andrews. James Andrews' grandfathers were William Andrews and William Dorling, whom I have already mentioned. The latter was a successful printer in Epsom back in 1821. Henry Dorling succeeded him and became Clerk of the Course and well-known for the Dorling Race Cards. The Dorling name, through Henry Mayson Dorling and the Rev. Earle Dorling, was prominent in the town till quite recently. I had many dealings with Dorling & Co. which was, in fact, eventually taken over by Pullinger's, themselves having already absorbed Birch & Whittington some time earlier.

Henry Dorling was well off, and lived at Ormonde House, a fine establishment at the eastern end of the High Street between what is now Fads and the railway bridge. The house disappeared after the 1859 railway extension. Dorling's second wife was Elizabeth Mayson, whose daughter by her first husband, Isabella, was to become much more widely known.

Henry and Elizabeth, who already had eight children between them, produced a further thirteen, and moved to live in the 1828 Grand Stand, which he owned, on the race course. This provided more space for that enormous and apparently very noisy family.

Isabella married a successful publisher and old family friend of the Dorlings. His name was Sam Beeton. Better known as Mrs. Beeton, Isabella died at the very early age of twenty eight, but in a comparatively short time had, with the help and encouragement of husband and step-father, produced that prestigious work, 'The Book of Household Management', usually known, of course, as 'Mrs. Beeton's'.

The present Fads building will be better remembered by many Epsomians as Coppens, that remarkable shop so popular for so long. It was Thomas' when I was little. The very mention of the name 'Coppens' by me during my various talks on the town in recent years brings forth 'oohs' and 'aahs' from the ladies.

o 0 o

I have already referred to Lord Rosebery, whose name seemed to crop up rather a lot in my early years. I only once remember seeing him, and that was driving through the town in his open carriage with his little grand daughter Primrose by his side, and with two postillions riding behind. Just imagine postillions surviving into the third decade of the twentieth century. I believe my father met him only once, and that was in 1894 when, as Prime Minister, he visited Christ Church on Epsom Common and presented each of the choirboys with a shilling.

Our firm supplied His Lordship with coal for the Durdans, but that would have been dealt with by one of his minions. That was not the case, however, with Major General Northey of Woodcote, another Epsom notable, who would personally invite my father in for a glass of sherry when placing his order. Etiquette from another era.

The Northey family lived at Woodcote House from the time of Sir Edward Northey (1651–1723), who was Attorney General in the reigns of William the Third, Queen Anne, and George the First. He was knighted by Queen Anne, who granted him an annuity of £1500.

The house, originally in beautiful Queen Anne style red brick, was partly rebuilt in Victorian times and became somewhat less attractive. This still stands today and is now divided into flats. I am told an interesting feature was once the large ice house constructed underground where part of Worlds End now is. Ice was brought from Norway in winter to fill this huge store place. The large estate was originally acquired by Edward Northey in the very early eighteenth century from Lord Baltimore, who at one time owned all that is now the RAC Park, The Durdans and the land developed, as I have already stated, by Harwood's in the 1930s. During the Second World War the army took over the building, and by all accounts did not treat it too well after the Northey family finally left in December 1939.

During the nineteenth century the family was still playing its part in the life of Epsom and of the nation. One member, E. R. Northey, who fought in the Battle of Waterloo at the age of nineteen, became a most distinguished soldier and eventually High Sheriff of Surrey. The Northey family still possesses the amazingly well written diary in which he describes his travels in Portugal and Spain, when a young Ensign, on his way to join Lord Wellington.

I note with interest that he was a member of the Local Health Board in Epsom when my great grandfather was its Rent Collector. His son was the much respected Rev. E. W. Northey (1832–1914), educated at Eton and Corpus Christi, a Surrey County Councillor taking great interest in elementary and secondary education. He was also Lord of the Manor of Ewell, Cuddington and Cheam.

My own particular memory of the Northeys is of one of our regular customers in the 20s and 30s – the dapper Major General Sir Edward Northey (known as 'Eddie'). A rosy face, a military moustache, a straw boater, a monocle and a cane – 'the very model of a modern Major General' in fact. Sir Edward went to Eton and Sandhurst, was an excellent all-round sportsman, who regrettably lost an eye playing polo in Kenya. He served in South Africa from 1897.

His grandson, Martin, whom I have met recently, is the current Lord of the Manors of Ewell, Cuddington and Cheam.

Archibald Philip Primrose became Lord Dalmeny at the age of four, upon the death of his father in 1851, and became the fifth Earl Rosebery in 1868 on the death of his grandfather.

At Eton in the early sixties his classics master, Mr. Johnson, wrote of him at various times – 'singularly well-informed . . . knowledge of history considerable . . . rather over-educated and unnaturally intelligent . . . original . . . flippant . . . sarcastic . . . frivolous . . . witty . . . might become a poet.'

Politics and the Turf (though not necessarily always in that order) became his great interests. He is said to have had three ambitions – perhaps just a joke that became a legend – one, to marry an heiress; two, to become Prime Minister; three, to win the Derby. He married Hannah Rothschild in 1878 and became Prime Minister in 1894. His horse, Ladas, won the Derby that same year.

The wedding in 1878 was enthusiastically celebrated by the locals with much jingo-junketing, ale and sandwiches, pies and Union Jacks, and even two huge garlands right across the High Street. That is something that would not get planning permission today. Hannah, who was a very large lady, he would amusingly and irritatingly describe as 'considerable'.

Of his premiership he said, 'There are two supreme pleasures in life. One is ideal, one is real. The ideal is when a man receives the seals of office from his sovereign. The real pleasure is when he hands them back.' He was the last Prime Minister to have been younger than John Major.

As for Derby winners, he had two more – Sir Visto and Cicero. They are buried in the Durdans grounds, with Ladas, at the top of Worlds End.

His keen interest in local affairs is evidenced by the fact that for a few years from 1899 he was a member of the Town Council. Rosebery Park was his gift to Epsom for 'children and dogs to roam free.' The roaming free of dogs is now controversial.

In 1874, when he was negotiating for the purchase of The Dudans, estate agents told him that this was the best place in the kingdom to hear the nightingale. He moved in in 1878 – and when did he hear his first nightingale? 1899!

The first Durdans, which may have stood on slightly different ground, was built about the year 1640, and it would be here, with Lord Berkeley, that Charles the Second dined after killing a stag in 1664, as Samuel Pepys recorded. Lord Berkeley told the Duchess of Devonshire of his 'great honour' and that they were 'very merry and in excellent spirits'. A merry evening with the Merry Monarch.

When Nonsuch Palace was being demolished after years of neglect by Barbara Villiers, Lady Castlemaine, it was Lord Berkeley in the late 1670s and early '80s who was authorised to remove building materials, and much went into the new Durdans in Chalk Lane.

It was in 1881 that Lord Rosebery built the Riding School. This large red brick building right on Chalk Lane has a floor area of nearly nine hundred square yards. It is a really fine building and it is good to know it is now being preserved and not, as at one time feared, demolished.

In 1689 George Berkeley sold The Durdans to Sir William Turner for £3450 and he, in turn, sold to the Duke of Argyle in 1708. By 1711 it was in the possession of Lord North. In 1726 an advertisement appeared, stating that Durdans was 'to be lett'. From about 1737, for the next ten years, Frederick, Prince of Wales, father of George the Third, took up residence. Lord Rosebery's diary mentions payments made by the Prince to his Housekeeper of £100 per annum, and to his Watchman of £12. 10. 0. for half a year's work.

There is a story that Prince Frederick, walking out from The Durdans one day, came across a chimney sweep intruding upon his grounds. The man, upon being told to be off, not only stood his ground but removed his coat, challenging the Prince to a fight. Not daunted, the latter likewise removed his coat. The fight proved to be somewhat one-sided, with the heir to the throne soon on the ground. Having acknowledged defeat and rewarded the victor, he subsequently had erected on the spot a flint obelisk to mark the occasion. This was eventually demolished, and it is said the flints were incorporated into the new parish church. The location of the obelisk must have been somewhere around the lower end of the present Downs Road, where at one time a grove of walnut trees leading to The Durdans ended. We have today a Walnut Close in the estate of comparatively new houses between Downs and Burgh Heath Roads.

By 1747 the owner of The Durdans was William Belchier. It would be during his time that it burnt down in February 1755, to be replaced by the present building. *The Times* contained an advertisement for its sale in 1815, after it had been purchased by a Mr. Blackman, who finally sold it in 1819 to Sir Gilbert Heathcote for £8500. Sir Gilbert was succeeded by Mr. Arthur Heathcote. Their name in our town is perpetuated in Heathcote Road between Ashley Road and Worple Road; Ashley Road itself being named after a Mrs. Ashley, the owner of Ashley House for a long time. This dates from 1709.

Lord Rosebery's diary states, 'No wonder the house swarms with rats. One of the bedrooms was used as a corn loft,' and that the 'mad Lady Heathcote used to take refuge in the Grotto.'

In 1836 the land between Woodcote and The Durdans was sold to Sir Gilbert by Mr. Northey of Woodcote for £80.

From his lordship's diary I also learned that Epsom 'tooters' or 'touters' got their name from the people of Tooting, who used to waylay visitors on their journey to Epsom races on behalf of certain Epsom tradesmen to secure their custom. Hence 'touts'.

Lord Rosebery died at The Durdans on the twenty-first of May 1929. Having suffered terribly from insomnia all through his political life and afterwards, he would often drive round and round the Epsom and neighbouring roads hour after hour at night. Sadly his only son, Neil, had been killed in the war.

It was his younger daughter, Lady Sybil Grant, who then lived at The Durdans for a number of years. She was quite a character. She befriended the gypsies, sometimes dressing herself in the strangest of garbs and sometimes insisting upon living in a caravan. She, on occasions, travelled around the country, including the visiting of other 'stately homes', sitting in a specially made seat on top of a motorised caravan. She wrote poetry, took great interest in the theatre, and on several occasions visited my father in his dressing room at the Ebbisham Hall when he was appearing in musical shows, which she loved – provided it was not Gilbert & Sullivan, which she hated.

Just after the war, when I had more or less taken over the local society's productions, I was invited to The Durdans with the committee of the Epsom Operatic Society and some other performers, with husbands and wives. We duly arrived, importantly in dinner jackets and evening dresses, only to find Sir Charles Grant in a lounge suit. In a bit of a huff the poor chap was sent upstairs to change. In the course of a very strange evening, during which we were waited upon by some ancient and faded servants in some ancient and faded uniforms, 'Lady Sib', as we called her, asked me to perform with her in a short play she herself had written. All this came as a complete shock to me. My sight reading is bad enough but the play was worse. In some of my more light-hearted Epsom talks I have been able to boast that 'I am unique in having performed a home-made play with the red-headed daughter of a former Prime Minister when she was wearing a balaclava helmet made of sequins.'

The present residents of the famous house are Mr. and Mrs. Bruce McAlpine. They have changed the name, as Lord Rosebery had contemplated doing many a year before, back to just 'Durdans' of the seventeenth century. I am grateful to them for lending me the diary to which I have been referring.

o 0 o

1927 saw the move of Furniss' coal and corn merchants business from the original building in West Street to No. 100 High Street, where eventually as T. Furniss & Son Ltd., Coal Merchants, Oil Distributors and Garden Suppliers, my brother Bob and I carried on as Directors till we retired in 1983. The premises is now occupied by Linwood Strong, the Opticians. I am pleased to see that one of the mid-nineteeth century iron columns that used to support the large advertisement board – originally for G. & J. Furniss – across the entrance to the yard still survives.

My grandfather Thomas, as I have mentioned earlier, erected the West Street building himself in the early 1870s. To give it strength he embedded any metal he could lay his hands upon, such as old bicycles or old bedsteads, into the concrete. The walls are exceptionally thick and a considerable task awaits some future demolition man.

Thomas William, son of William Thomas, was born in 1828; and I must say I find it hard to believe that I had a grandfather who was born the year George the Fourth offered the Premiership to the Duke of Wellington. The 1841 census return shows him as a thirteen year old carpenter's apprentice living in Clay Hill.

Grandfather had a very long connection with Christ Church on the Common, which was founded by Elizabeth Trotter, daughter of James Trotter of Horton Manor. The first Christ Church, which dated from 1843, was what might be called 'a pretty little church'. It was in 1874 that a separate parish was formed and the new Christ Church was built two years later. This still stands amongst the trees, impressive both in its exterior and interior. The rood screen added later is particularly notable.

My uncle Tom, my father and my cousin Tommy were all choristers in their time. Grandfather was associated with the church from its building in 1876 till his death in 1908. There is a brass tablet there to his memory. All would approve of my making mention of George E. Good. He was an industrious and inspiring choirmaster and organist for many a long year.

Both my brother and I were baptised at Christ Church by the Rev. Henry Bowles, who followed the better known Canon Hunter as Vicar (1881–1911).

My oldest possession is the sailor hat I wore at Bob's christening in 1920. The name of the ship on the ribbon is 'H.M.S. Pinafore'.

Grandfather Thomas was but a young man of twenty-one when in 1849 he sailed for America. His father still had the family tailor's business at the Yew Tree Cottages, and he had five younger brothers. Perhaps he felt he might try his luck and make a new beginning in a new country, or perhaps have a little adventure whilst he was young.

In a letter, now brown and faded, which I still have, he speaks of the kindness he received in a foreign land, of his immediate employment as a builder, and of the birth of his daughter Sarah – my Auntie Sis (1853–1937). The letter is from Yonkers, a suburb of New York, dated 17th December 1854, and is addressed to his grandmother, Sarah, who was born in 1770 and married Thomas Furniss, the tailor of Epsom, in 1798.

After the American Civil War broke out, Grandfather found himself attached to the northern forces in the U.S. Sanitary Commission. I possess an envelope addressed to 'Mr. Furniss, care of Dr. Jenkins, Sanitary Commission, Washington D.C., U. States.' The postmark is dated February 1862. He certainly travelled south as I know that at one time he was a member of a Masonic Lodge in Louisiana. His period in the southern states would account for Aunty Sis' concern for the black people and in particular for those 'poor little piccaninnies' previously referred to.

I know nothing of my grandfather's wife in Yonkers, except that she was called Elizabeth and died some time in the 1860s. One can imagine the problems of his return to his native town – that long sea journey with little girls of about fourteen and six. The census return of 1871 shows him as a widower and corn merchant, living with his father, William, and mother, Mary Ann, brother Alfred, sister Frances and eleven year old daughter Elizabeth. Sis lived with his brother George next door. In the three Yew Tree Cottages (numbers 94, 96 and 98) there were at that time a total of seventeen members of the Furniss family.

Without a house of his own, Thomas quickly found that triangle of land in West Street, between the railway and what is now called Station Approach, and there built his home. One can now understand the Dutch influence in his architecture. New York had once been the Dutch New Amsterdam and he had doubtless built houses in this style in Yonkers. In 1899 he built a similar house in Temple Road. This still stands on the junction of Hazon Way divided into flats. I possess some very faded photos showing this building in progress, taken by my father when aged fourteen.

Thomas set up, as well as a builder, as Coal and Corn Merchant. He also worked a chalk pit near Reigate. A photo I have clearly shows in his shop window advertisements for American canned foods. He also brought across the Atlantic, it would seem, such Americanisms as 'I'm agin it', 'Don't be sassy', 'Well I'll be cussed' and many words and expressions that he always retained. He persisted in pronouncing America as 'Am-merry-key'.

In 1871 Thomas married Marianne Elliott, daughter of James Elliott of Malden, Surrey, a Beadle. At the time of her birth he was a police constable and she was called Mary Ann. Her death certificate of 1917 shows her as Marian. They had a son Thomas in 1872, a daughter Marian, known as May, in 1874, and the baby of the family, my father, William George, in 1885. They all lived with Sis and Lizzie in the large house, which also served as shop, stores and offices. The telephone number was Epsom 28. I first knew it as 228. When I started work it was 2288. Finally we had 22288. That's progress. To return to the Elliotts: My paternal grandmother's brother, another James, emigrated to Carnduff, Saskatchewan, Canada, and over a period of a hundred years his descendants have spread throughout both Canada and the United States. I am happy to say I am in contact with many of them.

Uncle Tom became father of Ruth, Margery and Tommy. He retired to Salcombe in South Devon in 1924. His father-in-law was a certain Sam Crocker, who had a dusty old fashioned shop selling leather goods, mainly specialising in horse harness, at the 'top' end of the High Street next to the Albion.

I well remember having to go to this quaint survival of Victorian days in the early 1930s to pay an account. Old Sam, wishing to present me with a proper receipt, turned to his equally ancient assistant – 'Where's my pen and ink?' he squeaked. After a pen and an enormous bottle of ink had been found and the necessary document laboriously written, he surprisingly started searching all around the shop – under the desk, upon shelves and in cupboards, while I stood there for what seemed ages. At long last he just handed me the paper with the words, 'Blot it yourself.'

Aunty May became a good painter – exhibiting from 1898 to 1940 at the Royal Academy, the Royal Institute, the Institute of Oil Painters and many venues around the country. She married the landscape, figure and portrait painter, William Shackleton. He was born in Bradford in 1872, where some of his works now hang in the City Gallery. He studied in Paris and Italy and became known for his romantic imagination. Probably inspired by Turner, some of his later works were especially colourful. He was a cousin of Shackleton, the explorer.

A distinguished Epsom artist of the same period was William (David) Birch, who was the Principal of the Epsom School of Art in Church Street. Their current premises are in Ashley Road – the same road, in fact, in which once lived the famous artist John Piper (educated at Epsom College). Another English artist of the early part of the present century, Augustus John, lived for a time, so I am told, in St. Martin's Avenue – but a few yards from my present home.

Particularly exciting for me at the old West Street building was the chance to send wheat, oats, barley or maize crashing down pipes from the first floor stores into the appropriate bins in the shop. This operation, needless to say, filled the shop with a choking dust. There was also the excitement of the chaff-cutting machine. Coal was unloaded from a small siding on the railway, which could accommodate four trucks at a time, to be dropped down to the lower yard level on to the coal carts – or later one ton Ford lorries. Up to the time of nationalisation about a dozen railway wagons with FURNISS – white on a red background on a six- sided 'logo' – could be seen from time to time. There were also the stables for two or three cart horses. All this was fitted into the small triangle of land that can be seen today.

In the office Mr. Coombs reigned supreme. An ex schoolmaster, 'Coombo' had the most perfect handwriting imaginable and a very precise mind to go with it. Figures in the huge ledgers were exactly under each other, perfectly spaced. Totals were ruled off in exact lengths, one thin red line above a slightly thicker one. Unfortunately he was not so tidy in the matter of cigarette smoking, letting each burn down to turn his white whiskers orange. He would blow the ash in a series of little puffs till it fell to the brown lino floor. He would not have approved of calculators. His son Donald was an amateur actor with a particularly good speaking voice.

When 1927 came with the move to 100 High Street, it was a Mrs. Wright who took over the shop and part of the downstairs as a tea room. Wright's Restaurant subsequently moved to be next to us in the High Street in the 1930s, when Brad Furniss died. Much later, numbers 96 and 98 became the Yew Tree Restaurant, which is now called 'Le Jardin des Amis'. The West Street building is now divided into smallish flats and shops, an Employment Agency occupying the main position on the corner.

# *Chapter Three*

Sutton Valence School stands right on the edge of the hill to the south of Maidstone, overlooking the Weald of Kent. A beautiful location. I am sure my parents had to make considerable sacrifices to send me in 1929, and Bob a little later, to spend four important years of our lives there.

The place had a strong atmosphere of discipline and ritual about it, as such establishments do, but at the same time a feeling of friendliness and security. Somehow mathematics or Latin tended to be overshadowed by rugger or cricket in the enthusiasm of pupils and masters alike. I can still hear the crisp voice of Mr. Kay, 'There's nothing like the sharp crack of shoulder on thigh on a cold November aftrnoon.' The Headmaster, known as 'The Old Man', was once referred to by an old boy as 'an insipid cleric'. There was nothing insipid, however, about the sadistic vigour the Rev. William Wyatt Holgate displayed when he pronounced the dreaded words, 'Come here boy, I'm going to beat you.' That form of punishment was neither illegal nor frowned upon. The masters, I was told, like to be known as 'Schoolmasters' and not 'Teachers'. Teaching was hardly the strong suit of the majority of them, I rather agreed.

My major sporting achievement (academically – not a lot) was to be runner-up in the half mile and the cross country races. Second best was no disgrace, even if the victor was but a shy little boy with big glasses. My closer and longer association with the great runner, Sydney Wooderson, came a few years later. In class I often sat next to his brother, Stanley, and to this day we have never agreed whether it was he who got me into trouble by talking too much or vice versa.

At Christmas 1930 I played the part of Mrs. Fulverton Fane in the school play, 'The Fourth Wall'. The programme, which I still have, shows the part of Major Fothergill being taken by a certain C. B. Groves. Sir Charles, the conductor, I am pleased to say, during the period he was the Musical Director of the English National Opera, came to see my productions at the Epsom Baths Hall, and became a Vice President of the Nonsuch Opera Society, with which I have been so intimately associated for well over twenty years.

After I left the school the Chairman of the Governors was A. F. S. Cotton, a name well-known in Epsom. He followed his father, A. R. Cotton, both Arthurs, at the head of the firm of solicitors at the White House in Waterloo Road. I knew the firm firstly as Theodore Bell, Cotton and Curtis, and somewhat later as Cotton, Gumersall and Palmer.

My father would normally deal with a Mr. Burl, who was the long serving Chief Clerk. His son, Reg Burl, in my time, had an interesting little book and print shop in South Street. 'Come in and browse around' the sign suggested – hence 'Browser Burl'. He has kindly lent me a number of old books and programmes to study.

The White House was reputed by some to have been the home for a short time of the Prince of Wales (later George the Fourth) and Mrs. Fitzherbert, but there appears to be no reliable confirmation of this. The Prince was greatly disliked by his father and was in a financially very poor state about the time.

A former resident was certainly Sharon Turner, the nineteenth century historian and philosopher, of whom C. J. Swete says in his 1860 'Handbook of Epsom' – 'a master of the very purest English idiom'. His 'History of England' ran into twelve volumes.

A. F. S. Cotton, who has been most kind in supplying local information and jogging my memory, was for a number of years Clerk to the Magistrates, and also served on a panel for law reform under no less than Lord Hailsham.

Arthur senior co-operated with the archaeologist A. W. G. Lowther around 1926-1928, when the latter discovered by chance what proved to be a Roman tile in a rabbit hole in Ashtead Oaks, on the far side of Epsom Common. It was during the period when A. R. Cotton was Lord of the Manor that the site was explored and found to be a 1st century Roman villa. Tiles, flues, hypocaust, ornaments and bath annexe were all discovered, but owing to lack of funds (where have we heard that before?) the work had to be abandoned.

It was Lowther who, as Secretary of the Surrey Archaeological Society about 1930, made the first move in the plan to excavate the site on Nonsuch Palace, though it was to be some twenty-eight years before this actually happened.

I have a roundabout family connection with Arthur Cotton, in that the sister (Maggie) of A. R. Cotton's wife (Hilda) married my father's first cousin, Alf Furniss. Alf and Maggie lived at Yew Tree Cottage (No. 98) till his death in 1946, and she continued there till it became part of the present restaurant. Their lovely little cottage garden, filled with the scent of phlox, then became a car park filled with the smell of cooking fat from the kitchen's extractor fans.

o 0 o

It was during the 1930s school years that the population of Epsom and District increased dramatically. The house building in Epsom by Roll's and Harwood's, in particular, I have referred to. Thousands of new houses sprang up around

Ewell. The name 'Stoneleigh' was now being heard. First Stoneleigh Station appeared, isolated in the middle of fields. Then road after road was built virtually connecting Epsom to Worcester Park.

When I first travelled on the old No. 70 bus from Epsom to Tooting in the mid-1920s it was, apart from a few landmarks like The George at Morden, fields all the way as far as the present South Wimbledon Underground Station. Gordon Home in 1901 goes as far as to say 'it is an exceptionally pretty highway at all seasons of the year.' Not very 'pretty' now. Soon all of what were once Henry the Eighth's Great and Little Parks vanished, leaving only Nonsuch Park, which thankfully still survives for our pleasure today.

Ewell Court estate sprang up on the other side of the Kingston Road.

o 0 o

I imagine Epsom people tend to take less interest in the history of Nonsuch Palace than they might because not a stone now remains above ground. There is nothing visible to excite the imagination. It was during the time I was closely connected with the Epsom Protection Society, and met enthusiasts also from the Archaeological Society, that I – for the first time – acquired some knowledge of what was once such a remarkable place.

Henry the Eighth's last and largest palace was begun in 1538 and within a comparatively short time Nonsuch became famed world wide for its size and its splendour. One hundred and forty-five years later it was being demolished. Information concerning its size, its lay-out and even its exact position, was for years all but lost, and what remained in the memory and records was widely conflicting and clearly inaccurate.

John Dent, one time Borough Librarian of Epsom & Ewell, was a man who felt compelled to find the truth and explore the palace. This he did, assisted by the writing of Cloudesley Willis – 'A Short History of Ewell and Nonsuch' 1948 – and excavations under his enthusiastic leadership began in July 1959. Four months later, when it was apparent that all possible information had been acquired and recorded, the site was filled in. Summer 1960 saw the exploration of the site of the Banqueting Hall (near the Ewell By-Pass). The history of Nonsuch and of the excavations is set out in great detail in Dent's 'In Quest of Nonsuch' 1962 – revised 1970. A special exhibition was mounted in 1988, the 450th anniversary of the commencement of the building. One might point out that the existing Nonsuch Mansion should not be confused with the palace, and is less than two hundred years old. Had not that wanton woman, Barbara Villiers, Lady Castlemaine, Duchess of Cleveland and King's mistress, through an extravagant life style, leading to gambling and debt, shown no interest in the Monarch's priceless gift of Nonsuch, other than the money that could eventually be squeezed out of it, Epsom and Ewell might now possess a tourist attraction of Hampton Court proportions.

o 0 o

Most of the new 1930's dwellings had coal-burning open grates and either anthracite or coke-burning boilers, so merchants like ourselves had a considerably increased market. The snag was that, whereas a three-ton load in Epsom in the 1920s might be destined for three or four customers, in Stoneleigh in the 1930s it could involve as many as twenty or more 'drops'. The cost of distribution and the office work connected with orders and payments became enormous and out of all proportion, especially as competition between so many merchants kept retail prices absurdly low. It was actually over thirty years before the merchants came to their collective senses and got to grips with the problem.

Once a week our Manager, Lindsay Hart, and I would trudge around the new Stoneleigh houses, which included going up and down Stoneleigh Park Road. I wonder which of us knocked upon the door of a certain Mrs Osborne? Her son John, who would have been seven years old in 1936, was destined to come suddenly into prominence, some years later, the day he wrote 'Look Back In Anger'.

Late in the 1950s goods yards began to close one by one, following the Dr. Beeching era when the railways were 'rationalised', as they termed it. So far as our business, managed by myself and my brother Bob since the end of the war when our father retired to South Cornwall, was concerned, we had to close our yards at St. Helier, Tattenham Corner, Banstead and Ashtead over a period of about twenty years. Finally, of course, it was the turn of Epsom.

In 1963 a mechanised coal depot – called Colmec – was erected at Tolworth for the use of a large number of merchants. The choice of fuels became limited, but loading was comparatively simple and quite speedy. The great saving was in the elimination of the fuel lost. When coal was landed, that is, thrown out of a truck on to the ground and subsequently picked up, as much as ten per cent could vanish, including pilferage and degradation. At Colmec every ton to be delivered by the merchant was all that was loaded and charged to him.

Unfortunately it was getting late in the day. The public began to give up solid fuel fires and to use gas for central heating, so as each ton had now, at last, become more profitable, the number of tons were steadily decreasing. The 1970s saw a big decline. By the time we retired in 1983 the business was but a sad shadow of the good (?) old days. Colmec itself finally had to close in 1988. These days one hardly ever sees a coal lorry in Epsom at all.

Our last and largest oil tanker has, however, continued to be of service though under varying colours. It is still driven by Cyril Pawsey, who must now be classed as one of Epsom's 'characters'.

o 0 o

1929, as well as marking my debut at boarding school, also marked my debut on the stage – the first of eighty-nine amateur theatrical productions I have been involved in.

The Epsom Operatic Society, after a long gap from the outbreak of the Great War till the building of a suitable venue in the town, was now able to re-form and I, on holiday from school, was cast as 'Tommy Stanley', the Midshipman, in 'The Geisha'. We opened on December the thirty-first 1929, which means I have just (and only just by four hours) been in Epsom theatricals during eight different decades.

The venue was the new Ebbisham Hall in Ashley Road, which was connected to the Myers Hall at its rear. In the recent developments the shell of the Ebbisham Hall has been retained. The exact site of the stage is now the magazine and newspaper part of Menzies.

Unfortunately the stage, despite my father's pleadings with J. G. Beaumont, was not only very shallow, but made most difficult for staging by odd shaped partitions, steps and ceilings. J. G. Beaumont and Henry Myers, who gave his name to the small hall – perpetuated today at the Epsom Playhouse – insisted that the building was planned and erected primarily for the use of the Epsom Brotherhood; although, of course, 'others could hire it if they so wished.' Over the course of the next fifty-three years very many 'others' did so wish. The Ebbisham Hall not only housed operatic and dramatic productions, but public and private meetings, jumble sales, church services, the army during the war, dances, parties, trade fairs, exhibitions, blood donating and various charity functions. That multi-purpose hall is much missed today but leaves very many happy memories.

In the orchestra pit for 'The Geisha' was the violinist, George Bixley, who had even been billed as 'Master' Bixley in his earlier days. He married Kathleen Riddick in 1934. Kathleen was the daughter of Charles Riddick of Station Road. Many an Epsom home or office had a clock with the name 'Riddick' upon it. There was even one just below the Royal Box on the Grand Stand. 'Charlie', who had a good bass voice and had been in many a concert, was also the conductor of The Epsom Brotherhood Orchestra. On one occasion when he was ill, the fourteen year old Kathleen had taken over the baton. She studied 'cello, piano and composition at the Guildhall School of Music. In 1933 she, with George Bixley, formed the Surrey String Orchestra that in 1944 became the Surrey Philharmonic Orchestra. In the same year the London Womens' String Orchestra (the first professional all womens' orchestra), which she also founded, became the Riddick Orchestra. The Surrey 'Phil.' went from strength to strength, attracting famous guest conductors and famous guest soloists. Kathleen, in 1951, was the first woman to conduct at the then new Royal Festival Hall. In 1961 she was awarded the OBE. In 1973 she died. George Bixley, I am pleased to say, has recently provided me with useful information both musical and otherwise.

Sir Humphrey Millford founded the Epsom Choral Society in the 1920s and his son Robin, a composer, became its first conductor. He lived in St. Martin's Avenue. In time William Cole succeeded him. That was before the days of Richard Fentiman already mentioned. The Epsom Choral Society was formed to take part in the Leith Hill Music Festival, whose inspiration and father figure was the great Ralph Vaughan Williams. During the last war, when the Dorking Halls were not available, Vaughan Williams actually conducted at Epsom's St. Martin's Church.

With my earlier years at the Ebbisham Hall I remember one Jimmy Wall of the Epsom Herald – its first editor. He wrote the criticisms of the local shows, and would frequently refer to someone's performance as 'adequate'. What a useful word! His wife Iris, who died quite recently aged ninety-one, was closely connected with the Epsom Literary Society, which was founded as long ago as 1849. She was highly knowledgeable about local affairs and a much respected Epsomian.

It has always seemed to me dubious whether written criticisms of local amateur shows, once they are all over, are really useful or desirable. Reports would be a different matter, as would, of course, be appreciations or adjudications by an acknowledged expert for instructional purposes. Even if the writer were experienced and knowledgeable there should surely be sufficient space devoted to allow the criticism to be both comprehensive and balanced.

A standard is hard to establish; consistency even harder to achieve. Criticism of the performing arts presents a basic problem. Acting, singing, dancing and playing do not stand still to be scrutinised and analysed. They are on the move; disappearing into thin air at the very moment of their creation. A critic can only write what can be remembered later, of what the impression was, of what something appeared to be.

My knowledge of the history of local theatrical organisations takes us back to 1904. That year a man called Sydney Drake ran a small pierrot troupe performing at the Victoria Hall in Leatherhead's High Street. This included Amy Pearman, Bill Higgs (pianist) and my father, an absolute though very enthusiastic novice of nineteen. One night C. E. Grantham, the stage scenery designer, builder and painter, went to a performance. 'Not bad' was his comment – good enough at any rate for him to use the troupe as a nucleus of the Leatherhead Operatic Society he formed. They opened with 'HMS Pinafore' in 1906 and continued at the Victoria Hall – later used as a cinema – and Epsom's Ebbisham Hall, the Crescent Cinema in Leatherhead, and currently perform at the Thorndike Theatre and the Epsom Playhouse.

The little Victoria Hall saw the infancy of the professional Leatherhead Repertory Company, which under the leadership of Hazel Vincent Wallace created the Thorndike Theatre on the Crescent's site.

Charlie Grantham was a brilliant scenic artist. A very early memory of mine is of visiting his studio in Hylands Road, Leatherhead. His painting was of the realistic style of his time. A bank of roses looked like a bank of roses – you could almost smell them.

My earliest theatre memory is of 'Merrie England' at the Victoria Hall in 1920. At the age of four and a half I stood on the stage and decided I liked it.

In 1929 Amy Higgs was still prominent in local entertainment, and in fact she was to be seen in the town actively engaged in womens' clubs till the age of ninety-four. Bill Higgs was the Musical Director and my father still the leading figure in productions, both as performer and producer. Popular as light comedian was Reg Johnson, who ran a greengrocer's shop just beyond the railway bridge in East Street on the right. During the war Reg was in charge of our food rationing, and for as long afterwards as rationing continued. His office was at the Foresters Hall in Waterloo Road. This hall is no more and the site utilised in conjunction with the indoor market on the old Page Motors land.

The history of the Epsom Operatic Society actually goes back to the 1911–1914 period at the Epsom Public Hall built in 1883. This was on the corner of the then Station Road and Church Street; now the Quadrant. This building had a rather elaborate front (Gordon Home said 'flamboyant') and like the adjacent Technical Institute in Church Street, which still survives, was of brightish red brick. This latter was once the home of the Epsom School of Art and Design, now in a modern building in Ashley Road.

My father first tried his hand as producer in 1912. The Public Hall became the Palladium Cinema in 1916, and it was here I first experienced the 'moving pictures' – Mary Pickford and Charlie Chaplin. Herbert Glenister, the Manager, was a popular local musician, versatile on the Palladium piano, in dance bands and at social functions.

I possess the programme of the Ebbisham Masonic Lodge's Ladies Festival of 1922, when Charles Riddick was the Worshipful Master and music was provided by 'Mr. H. Glenister's Orchestra'. The menu is interesting and would defeat most of today's participants:

*Whitstable Natives*
*Hors d'Oeuvres*
*Clear Real Turtle*
*Fillets of Dover Sole Caprice*
*Calves Sweetbreads and Spinach*
*Saddle of Southdown – Red Currant Jelly – Chateau Potatoes*
*Punch Romaine*
*Roast Pheasant in Casserole Singapore*
*Salad*
*Pears in Port Wine*
*Ice Bombs*
*Petit Fours – Dessert – Coffee*

'Pa' and 'Ma' Glenister were also closely connected with the Leatherhead Operatic Society, as was their daughter, Maudie, whom I first remember standing next to me in 'The Geisha'. Much later she became our Mayor's secretary at the Town Hall for quite a number of years till she died in that horrible disaster at Rijeka in Yugoslavia, when a plane packed with holidaymakers caught fire on the ground.

The Palladium was demolished in 1934, once the 'talkies' were established at the Capitol just opposite.

'Lovers of wholesome entertainment – those who lead busy lives and need relaxation – we hope will find in this theatre a centre where their accumulation of domestic and business anxieties will be forgotten.' So said the management of the very modern and very large Capitol Cinema in 1929. The theatre had a seating capacity of just over 1500. There was also a large cafe which was let out for functions and where I enjoyed quite a few happy evenings. At one time there were Sunday Band Concerts on the stage, and I have recently met someone who well remembers Billy Cotton and Jack Hylton at the Capitol. In 1947 it became The Granada. In 1960 it closed. Keymarket, Maples and Allied Carpets have all occupied the site in more recent times.

Of the Odeon Cinema I write later, but here are a few brief points concerning the Electric Cinema and the Cinema Royal, both of which opened in 1910. (Anyone requiring really detailed information on our old Epsom cinemas should read Trevor White's 1989 booklet on the subject.)

The Electric Cinema stood at the junction of Hook Road and East Street. In 1926 under Tommy Little it became known as the Pavilion Theatre and was used for live shows, but the venture was a failure from the outset and it closed in 1929. I particularly remember the posters advertising Escapologists and such-like Music Hall turns. It was, however, a further twenty-four years before it was demolished and its twin domes vanished from the scene.

The Cinema Royal was next to the old Boots shop on the one side and the railway bridge on the other. It was there I first saw a 'Western' and it cost 4d. 'Top Hat' some ten years later still cost under a shilling. It had been some seven years earlier that I had been taken to the Princes Theatre in London (now for some reason called the Shaftesbury) to see someone reputed to be 'a rather good young American dancer'. I was fortunate, therefore, to have seen Astaire in the flesh before he achieved legendary status. The Cinema Royal closed in 1938.

From very much earlier times there was a long vanished playhouse, run by a Mr. Powell in Hudsons Lane, which is believed by some to be more or less where Waterloo Road is now. In that period there was a theatrical company managed by Mrs. Mynn. She was using part of the Spa buildings – probably the New Tavern – in 1708.

o 0 o

When you leave school you can suddenly find yourself transformed from a biggish fish in a tiny pool to just a tiddler in the sea. I never really settled down to work at Clarkes Business College in Chancery Lane, and by the summer of 1934 knew as much – if not more – about London's streets and theatres as I did of typewriting and accountancy. The latter did, however, stand me in good stead in years to come.

By the autumn I was working in the Upper High Street coal yard – unloading trucks and loading lorries. I wonder how many people realise how black from head to toe one gets when working with coal, especially in dry weather when the coal dust gets in everywhere – into the hair, up the nose and between the toes. At one time not many coalmen would have baths to go home to. I got £1 a week from T. Furniss & Son Ltd. (as the firm had been styled since 1932), and it was not just a 9 to 5 job for five days a week. It was 8 to 6 for five and a half days. Proper coalmen probably got £4.10.0. a week, plus some commission for 'odd sacking' – that is, selling coal from their lorries for cash; 'hawking' on prescribed 'rounds'. These references to 'coal' include, of course, house coals, anthracites, coke and patent fuels such as ovoids and coalite.

My hobbies during these years both involved the use of my legs – Running and Dancing. With Sydney and Stanley Wooderson I had joined Blackheath Harriers on leaving school, and we frequently trained together, usually on Tuesday and Friday evenings or on Sunday mornings, on the old three-laps-to-a-mile track at Battersea Park or the new London University ground at Motspur Park. Our trainer was Albert Hill, the victor of both the 800 metres and 1500 metres at the 1920 Olympics.

I was also in the chorus of the Epsom Operatic Society's shows and took dancing lessons, creating the exciting experience of twice taking part in revues at Wimbledon Theatre. I had the use of a little Austin Seven at the time and recall, with some sense of shame and some of bravado, coming home from one performance giving a lift to seven girls at once, including two sticking through the sunshine roof.

In 1934 I won – to everyone's surprise including mine – the Surrey Junior Half Mile, and by 1938 I had actually been chosen once for the County, although in a minor fixture, and once represented the A.A.A.

However, this was very small stuff compared with the growing fame of my training companion, who by 1937 had won the National Mile title three times and broken the British Record twice. I was on holiday in Cornwall in August when it was confidently expected he would do so for a third time. On the Saturday evening of my return I at once telephoned Sydney to find out how he had got on. With typical modesty, a quiet voice just said 'I broke the World Record.' The rest, as they say, is history.

Amateur athletics was really amateur in those days. Not a penny was paid. Training had to be fitted into any spare time that could be found. Tracks were made of cinders, often very rough, and much slower to run on than the high-tech plastic surfaces of today. There was no TV and no showy 'lap of honour'.

To instance how very amateurish it was: on one occasion at quite an important meeting in a relay race we used our rolled up evening papers – there were no batons. At another, the Club's Two Mile Steeplechase Championship, we had to climb over the public park's iron railings – there were no hurdles – and in any case the course was nowhere near two miles. Once in the final of the A.A.A. Steeplechase at The White City stadium, I realised afterwards that we had certainly run well over the correct distance – by about seventy yards, I thought. I proved this beyond all doubt to the A.A.A. authorities and received a reply, weeks later, which virtually said 'Oh well, it doesn't matter'. And that was our National Championship.

Wooderson was now a household name, featuring sometimes in cartoons in the daily press, comedians' patter, and even in a Western Brothers' (Kenneth and George) song. On the twentieth of August 1938 I was honoured to be chosen to act as pacemaker for the first lap of his attack on the Half Mile and 800 metres World Records. My mother and father, hearing about it on the wireless and seeing my name in rather large letters in The Daily Express that morning, were in a more nervous state than I was. Needless to say they were delighted, as well as relieved, by the successful outcome.

o 0 o

The offices of the old EUDC were at Bromley Hurst in Church Street. I still remember my father's words in a topical song in 'A Country Girl' at the Ebbisham Hall in 1932, '. . . though I'm glad we're not cursed, with some like Bromley Hurst, in the beautiful Valley of Bong.' The joke, which seemed to be much appreciated, was partly due to the fact that the offices were always being complained of as unsatisfactory, but largely because E. G. Wilson, who owned Bromley Hurst, had just sold the building to the E.U.D.C., of which he was the Clerk.

The new Town Hall was opened on 10th March 1934 in The Parade and it is still our administrative centre. Over the years nearby buildings have been annexed. As I write this, a considerable new Town Hall extension is in the course of construction.

The Parade is no longer the quiet and attractive place I first knew. Like other parts of Epsom, it has become much changed at the hands of developers. The sixties and the seventies saw much demolition in our town leaving a number of unsightly and wasteful spaces. Originally called 'Church Parade', it was the walkway from the new spa town to the old centre by the Parish Church of St. Martin's, where people would 'parade' on Sundays. A few old buildings fortunately survive and outstanding is the little white cottage, No. 14, dated 1764.

People who regularly use the Parade these days will frequently recognise one of its residents – a tall man with the friendliest of smiles – without realising him to be one of our most distinguished Epsomians. Sir John Titman, who was recently knighted upon his retirement for his many years of service to Her Majesty, rose to be the Secretary to the Lord Chamberlain's Office in 1978 and became Serjeant-at-Arms to the Queen in 1982. His father, Sir George Titman, in his time, also became Secretary to the Office of the Lord Chamberlain.

The formalities of the Town Hall opening in 1934 included an address of welcome read by the Clerk to the Council, P. E. Whiteoak-Cooper, prayers led by the Vicar of Epsom, the Rev. Canon Pattison-Muir, the official opening performed by Lord Ebbisham and a vote of thanks by the Chairman, Councillor Harry Skelton, followed by tea for the various VIPs. Included in the last named was Sir Arthur Glyn, of an old and much respected Ewell family and a character of the day. I well remember him, always bent over at a considerably angle, pacing through the town and indeed the whole countryside at a great speed – and that despite his years. Also there was James Chuter Ede, who merits very special mention later.

The Ebbisham Hall for a short while in the 1930s housed the Epsom Little Theatre, run by Nigel Clarke. Plays were given for three evenings every other week during a short winter season. Nigel Clarke was a professional actor who gathered round him such professionals as himself, who were 'resting' – most of the time. His mother ran the Downs Hotel (now the Rubbing House) and poor Nigel was forced to spend much time behind the bar, which he hated. He was a disappointed actor, but it was a brave venture nevertheless.

The Epsom Gilbert & Sullivan Society also performed at the Ebbisham Hall about this time, but it did not have a very long history.

o 0 o

In the yard at the rear of 100 High Street were a number of old buildings in varying states of disrepair, the most interesting of which was the chapel. This red brick building, some sixty feet long, had been built in the eighteenth century and was finally demolished when Sainsbury's car park took its place in the 1980s. During the course of its existence it had been, for a period during the last century, the Epsom Methodists' first chapel before they moved to the Foresters Hall in Waterloo Road, and in 1915 to the present site in Ashley Road. It had also been a schoolroom and then for some long time G. & J. Furniss' paint shop and coffin shop. In its later years our T. Furniss & Son Ltd. used it as a store for corn and also for fertilisers.

It was either in the chapel or in one of the other dilapidated out-buildings, which included stables, that my father one day in the late 1930s made a discovery which at the time he realised as being of considerable interest to the family, but which in due course was to prove of more historical value than he imagined.

This was an old account book with yellowing pages and faded writing that was difficult to decipher, not so much on account of its age but of the scratchy scrawl of the handwriting, and most of all because many of the pages had been used both ways up with much writing between the lines. One way up it was clearly the account book of Thomas Furniss, a tailor, and written between the years 1820 and 1836. The other way round the accounts, in much neater writing, were in two parts – one in the 1720s and one during the 1750s.

Six or seven years ago I took this old book to Sean Kahn, the Curator of the Bourne Hall Museum in Ewell. This had been founded in 1969 and is now run by Jeremy Harte. At long last some expert examination was undertaken. This resulted in a book by Ina Godman, published by the Epsom & Ewell Borough Council in 1988 – 'The Furniss Journal 1728–1836'. Apart from the fact that it tells us something of Thomas Furniss and of his son, William Thomas (my great grandfather), and of many Epsomians at the time, its value is in the wealth of information it gives concerning the garments worn at the time, of materials, of repairs, of prices, and of changes in fashion.

To give some idea of the varied and interesting facts unearthed by Ina Godman, I here include a few extracts: 'The book must be about 260 years old as at least one page of hand-made paper bears the watermark of the 1720s, and the earliest entries are dated 1728–31. It is bound in parchment and once had two metal clasps, which have now vanished. Some of the pages were cut out and replaced by two folds of much later but still hand-made paper watermarked 1829 and 1830.'

Entries by a gentleman (1728–31) – 'A gallon of oyl 10/6', 'A horse £9.9.0' Brandy, by the way, seemed to cost 8/-d a gallon. Entries by a lady (1750s) – '14 yards Rich Poplin £1.15.0.', 'a pair of French finger gloves 2/-'. Her harpsichord hire was £2.12.6. with a further 7/6d for tuning. Materials mentioned by Thomas, the tailor, include Nankeen, Barragon, Kerseymore, Raised Flannel, Beaver, Toilinette, Shaloon, Drab, Dustian, Jean overalls, Valencia, Calimanco, Bannian, Back covers, Gambroon, Marsella, Hair Plush and Quilting between 1820 and 1836.

It is not clear how the book came into the possession of my great great grandfather. At the top of one page appears, 'In the year 1818 I planted several acorns' together with 'Emer Furniss', and three rather nice little drawings above 'C. Woods Gamecocks'. The book was then turned over and started from the other end. Inside this cover is a note in particularly good and bold copperplate, 'Take notice this book is to be kept clean and free from blots Wm. Thos. Furniss, Head Clerk' with just below added, 'G. F. Furniss, Under Clerk.' Thomas had been living at the Yew Tree Cottage for some twenty years, and William, his eldest son, in 1820 was a young man of eighteen. His instructions concerning blots were in vain I may add. It is most likely that he persuaded his old-fashioned parent to keep proper accounts and found the already ninety-year old book for this purpose. His brother, George Frederick, was at that time about fifteen, and probably added his name as a joke. William followed his father into the tailoring business and remained at the same address.

Amongst the customers of landowners, surgeons, parsons, attorneys, game-keepers, footmen, butlers, grooms and gardeners, were names still known in the town well into the twentieth century – Andrews, Bailey, Dearle, Jaquet and Trotter of Horton Place (now vanished and replaced by the gaunt tower of the mental hospital), for instance. There are many strange spellings. In one place a 'jacket' is written as 'jaquet', just after reference to Mr. Jaquet. The largest account in the book is that of Madame de Tessier. Between the years 1811 and 1848 she lived at Woodcote Park, a house dating from 1753 and one of the finest in Epsom and district. She seemed to spend a lot of money on her footmens' and coachmens' clothes. It is interesting to find that a jacket, waistcoat and breeches for a footman cost £6.6.0; that is to say the same as the first suit purchased from Bowden's for me when I left school in 1933.

Richard Evelyn (brother of the diarist, John Evelyn) was a former owner of Woodcote Park, purchased by the RAC in 1911. Following a big fire in 1935 the house had to be completely rebuilt. This was fortunately carried out to the original design. It creates a most imposing looking RAC Country Club and is a popular venue for functions.

The old book I have been describing is in a very delicate condition, but I am pleased to know that Ina Godman and the new curator of the Bourne Hall Museum, Jeremy Harte, have sent a transcription of its contents to the Costume Society who greatly value the information it contains. Articles have appeared in 'Costume' in 1989 and 1991.

According to photocopies of documents kindly given to me by Dr. H. L. Lehman, who has done so much detailed research into Epsom properties (Residential Copyholds of Epsom, 1988), Thomas Furniss, the tailor (1773–1847), first came into the picture as far as Yew Tree Cottage was concerned in 1801. My investigations into family history only began seriously when on leave during the war, when I spent a long time delving into records at St. Martin's Parish Church. What I found then, and subsequently, relating to the seventeenth and eighteenth centuries I will cover when I reach the 1940s period, but in the meantime the life of William Thomas Furniss will help to provide a little nineteenth century local history.

He was born in 1802 and married Mary Ann Marshall of Bristol. The marriage certificate I hold states they were married on the 30th September 1826, at Camberwell. He had seven sons (of whom another Thomas was my grandfather) and two daughters.

In 1848 the Public Health Act was passed, and Epsom became the first town in the country to have its own Local Health Board. This was in 1850 and includes the names of Jaquet (Postmaster), Langlands (subsequently Estate Agents), Bailey (Draper at Waterloo House), Northey (of Woodcote) and Harsant (the Chemist). It was just ten years earlier that gas light first came to Epsom. The site of the 1839 gasometer is still put to the same use today. In my possession is a receipt of 1871 headed 'Epsom Local Health Board' and made out to 'No. 303 The Literary Institution', with the name of William Thomas Furniss as 'Collector' printed at the bottom. He was also Parish Clerk for many years.

Great grandfather would have watched the demolition of the old Watch House with its stocks in the High Street, and the building of the present Clock Tower in 1849. This was at the time most controversial, particularly on account of its Chinese cupola. At one time it was suggested this exotic feature be removed – but of course it never has been. He would also have been a witness daily to the filling in of the pond which stood in the middle of the street, right in front of his home. This pond was egg-shaped and had posts around it but was considered insanitary by 1854. He would have been very familiar with the parish pump at the 'top' of the street.

The old book would appear to suggest that William Thomas in 1833–34, like his great grandfather John in the early eighteenth century, was the town's Constable. Entries in 1834 include 'cleaning out Watch House 2/6', 'straw for ditto 2/-'. The cost of spending all night with a man on suspicion of murder was 5/-. Apprehending a man at The Surrey Yeomen in Banstead, for stealing a shawl was 4/6. Taking fish out of Lodge Pond and breakfast for two prisoners seems only to have cost 9d. He died in 1874. His tomb is in the Parish Churchyard with his name and that of Mary Ann still quite clear.

The adjacent tombstone, that of his third and fifth sons, is unusual in that both perished in the same year and both under odd circumstances. The inscription states: 'In loving remembrance of Alfred and Frederick Furniss. Alfred whose death was caused by a runaway horse on the 5th of April 1871 was 35 years of age. Frederick who met an instant death by a locomotive engine on the 7th of November 1871 was 39 years of age. Lovely and pleasant in their lives and in their death they were not divided.'

o 0 o

Oscar Deutsch, whose Odeon company already owned some three hundred cinemas, came to Epsom on the 19th of April 1937 to open the Epsom Odeon. The outstanding feature of the exterior was the tower. The interior, accommodating about one thousand four hundred people, was most attractive, wide and not too deep, in soft pinks, greens and yellows.

Our yard being next door provided a good car park for the VIPs, and one of our coalmen, Bill, enthusiastically acted as car park attendant, doubtless looking for some good tips. Oscar Deutsch duly arrived with his little blonde wife and his large white Rolls. Epsom's stage stars, Tom Walls and Ralph Lynn, made their speeches, which we – perhaps unreasonably – expected to be very funny, but, as often happens, did not get the laughs they might have done had their scripts been provided by Ben Travers. Of the film shown I remember only that it was clearly not one that would be remembered – and isn't. Eventually there were drinks and much jolly chatting, during which Ralph Lynn actually said 'Good evening' to us. My only words from Tom Walls had come a few years earlier, when I was on duty in the coal order office and was not able to specify the exact time his fuel might be delivered. My poor excuses were greeted with a gruff and irascible, 'Just you send my bloody coal.'

Our expectant Bill stayed behind in the yard till late that night. Finally, the last to appear was the millionaire Oscar, who tottered towards his car, thrust his hand in his pocket, and with a patronising 'there-you-are-my-man' look emptied the contents into Bill's waiting hand and drove off. Bill looked down. It held 4½d!

The Odeon was a most pleasant cinema and very popular with Epsom people. Then the 50s and 60s saw the decline of the cinema everywhere. Our Odeon succumbed in June 1971, to stand there looking sad and empty before it was finally demolished to leave that depressing open space adjoining our yard.

For an unpleasant period it was occupied by gypsies. They moved in, blatantly driving their lorries, cars and caravans across the pavement, one morning; and despite the protestations of all the local shopkeepers and others, the authorities were quite unable to dislodge them. The whole area became absolutely filthy, although someone from the Council did occasionally come to sprinkle a white disinfectant powder around. Then one day, months later, they went as suddenly as they had come.

John Sharp, of Edwards and Sharp the Estate Agents, in the tiny building once a Boot and Shoe shop, continued to hold out and declined to sell that remaining small property on the High Street frontage, thus causing the large new Sainsbury's to be designed around it. This does have the effect of breaking up the line and perhaps keep our High Street more like its old self than might have been. John Sharp, who has now retired to the West Country, was at one time, I am told, President of the Rating Valuers Association. Other Epsomians I have known, who have occupied similar positions in their professions, include Ken Swiss, at one time President of the British Dental Association, and Phil Pullinger of the Booksellers Association.

o 0 o

'The Humble Petition of the Urban District Council of Epsom and Ewell for the grant of a charter incorporating the Urban District of Epsom and Ewell as a Municipal Borough' was made to 'the King's most Excellent Majesty in Council'.

Needless to say, the pros and cons were well aired in local papers and local bars. The verses I wrote at the time have been abandoned with similar junk in old files for the last fifty years:

'Our Councillors are thorough
And enthuse about a Borough
Quite impervious to all the fun we poke.
And the carrot used to urge us is
That we shall all be Burgesses
Instead of just a lot of simple folk.

'The fat, the old and balder men
Aspire to all be Aldermen
Ambition for the robe and chain inflate us.
Whilst our Borough Coat of Arms
Will depict our matchless charms
To exemplify our coming civic status.'

At noon on the 29th of September 1937 a grand ceremony took place in the High Street by the Clock Tower, at which the desired Charter was delivered into the hands of the Charter Mayor, Alderman J. Chuter Ede, JP, DL, MP, by Lord Ashcombe. I was fortunate enough to witness this from the upstairs front window of 100 High Street, together with parents, friends and a number of interesting bottles and tasty sandwiches. It was a colourful and memorable event.

A banquet (at which I was, needless to say, not a participant) took place at the Grand Stand in the afternoon, when James Chuter Ede responded to the toast. As was apparently the habit with that gentleman, the reply was fairly lengthy. A few extracts here will doubtless suffice. (I once, by the way, read some satirical verses on Epsomians that included the lines 'Those speeches we have in the Herald to read/And very long statements by James Chuter Ede.')

'Only three very ancient Boroughs in Surrey have a longer experience than ours in exercising urban powers' . . . 'Good wine needs no bush. The many excellencies of Epsom and Ewell need no public advertisements. The newspaper barons and billposters have reaped no fortune from urging the purchase of our infallible elixir. More expensive and less certain remedies for human ills have to be commended by grotesque pictures and descriptive letterpress creating new and more alarming symptoms, but never removing causes. Our name, unmentioned in the advertisement columns, remains a household word. Every medicine chest contains our sovereign remedy, which has cured more bad temper than all the other agencies of the world. Thus we enjoy a lifelong practical experience of the value of modest but continuous efficiency. Yearly, also, it is brought home to us that it is not the shouting at Tattenham Corner but the quiet figure in the judge's box which awards the Blue Riband. Today for us the "All Right" flag has been run up.' . . . 'In celebration of today let us not forget those who bred and trained us, and the affections and ambitions they had for this place and this people.' . . .

'With the addition of Ewell and Cuddington to our area in 1933, our civic life was reinvigorated with streams of fresh ideas, pulsing with determination to keep our equipment abreast of our needs and to provide adequately for the future.' . . . 'We feel that we are indeed, in the words of our Charter, "One Body Politic and Corporate by the name of the Mayor, Aldermen and Burgesses of the Borough of Epsom and Ewell" with perpetual succession. Whether we individually received our first mental grooming in the stables of Eclipse, or drank our first draughts of knowledge by the waters of the Roman Spring, or received our earliest instruction in any other of the public or private academies of this neighbourhood, or whether we came, in later life, to this ancient home of kings and this famous pleasure ground of peoples, we are united. So glorious a heritage as ours can borrow nothing from us. In dedicating ourselves to the service of this friendly Corporation, we are determined that, as our predecessors made it, we and our successors will keep it, growing and vital – None Such.'

My father always maintained he was a dunce at school. This was at Harry Newham's in The Parade, where he was taught most of the time by Alice Newham, of whom he became very fond and visited for many years afterwards. At the age of fourteen he left. Each dinner time the boys had to answer some question before they were allowed home. The only way they could get rid of Father was to ask the same question every day: 'How many half-crowns in a pound, Georgie?' 'Eight.' 'Right, off you go.'

He used to tell this tale when he spoke of that very bright little boy, Chuter Ede, who was three years his senior. He went to the Epsom National School in Hook Road, by the junction with East Street; now almost completely rebuilt in similar style but with a dash of Disney. A few people I have spoken to still remember C. W. Vasser being Headmaster there.

Jimmy Chuter Ede by all accounts certainly was a very 'bright little boy.' Son of an Epsom barber, James was born in Epsom in 1882. From the National School he went to Dorking High School till 1898 and thence to Christ College, Cambridge. By 1913 he was already President of the Surrey County Teachers' Association. During the war years he was in the East Surrey Regiment. He was a member of the E.U.D.C. and its Chairman, and soon the Surrey County Council and also its Chairman. He was elected a Member of Parliament in 1923 – for Mitcham and subsequently South Shields. After the Second World War he became a Privy Councillor and, under Attlee, Home Secretary from 1945 to 1951, and later Leader of the House. He became a Companion of Honour and finally elevated to the Upper House, not as Lord Ede but by a change of name as Lord Chuter Ede.

He had lived for eighty-three years in Epsom and in Ewell when he died there in 1965. A most outstanding Epsomian.

A newspaper cutting I have states that he was never an author but could 'express himself tersely'. He was a great reader with a love of Milton and Bunyan, 'with whom he was never quite out of sympathy.' It also states he was not musical. Funnily enough, the only time I ever met him was at a musical concert at the Ebbisham Hall. He certainly looked rather stern on that occasion. The cutting ends, 'through his career shone a constant love for his native town.'

# *Chapter Four*

It is said everyone knows where they were on the day Kennedy was assassinated. Likewise at eleven o'clock on Sunday September the third 1939 I suppose. We anxiously looked out over the Priesthill fields towards London half expecting to see bombs raining down on the city and the black smoke we had witnessed just three years earlier when the Crystal Palace was destroyed by fire.

Ron Harwood has reminded me it was his wedding day. He and his bride-to-be, Bunty, were confronted by the sight of Frank Lee on his bicycle shouting to them to take cover. Nothing happened. In fact, little happened for nine months. The Government even produced a little book, telling me how not to join the armed forces. Being employed in fuel distribution, I was one of the large number initially 'reserved' for the time being.

May 1940 changed all that and I found myself at Kingston Barracks and in the East Surrey Regiment. The long hot summer of that year was hectic for some, tragic for others, but for many like myself not immediately engaged or affected there was absolutely no feeling of history-in-the-making. It never appeared so exciting as it now does in films.

A few of us marched to Richmond Bridge and erected a rather pathetic coil of barbed wire across it. We began to dig a trench just outside Epsom towards Chessington and, before completing it, moved to commence another by the Drift Bridge, which we never finished either. We rehearsed 'cover from view' in Richmond Park, which involved lying down in the long grass for a chat or a smoke. The odd bomb did fall near the Vickers factory, but fortunately the damage was slight. The main effect of the bombing was that if the siren sounded before we went to the pictures we were confined to barracks, whereas if it sounded afterwards we were told to stay in the cinema. I was once in the Regal all night.

Some rather more serious exercises then followed in the tranquillity of the Isle of Man.

Upon my arrival in Dover in March 1941 the threat of invasion had come and gone. Within a matter of hours I had been reliably informed that the best place for morning coffee was The Creamery, and that the name of the usherette at the Odeon was Violet; of military matters not a word. One of my tasks became the maintenance and operation of a beach light at the land end of a long pier, known as the Eastern Arm (like millions of others I have embarked there holiday-wards many a time since). The theory was that should, under cover of darkness, a German be unwise enough to set foot at the other end he would be lit up and shot up. It was as well we never had to put this theory to the test as the beach light motor had to be started up by pulling a cord, as on motor mowers, and – as on motor mowers – it usually failed to work. There was some random bombing and some very optimistic shelling, but it was not the old 'Hell Fire Corner' any more and casualties were minimal.

I attended a so-called conference with General Montgomery. Of course there was actually no such thing as a 'conference' with Monty. He just spoke for hours on end, non-stop. I will always remember the opening: 'Gentlemen, there will be no coughing when I am speaking. You now have a minute to cough.' Then, looking at his watch, he gave the momentous order, 'Cough'. We obliged nervously. Finally he ordered us all to go for a two mile run before breakfast, and, eyeing those senior officers in the front row, said we had to keep fit 'not like those fat Brigadiers down there.'

On the subject of commanders, by the oddest of chances I once found myself sitting next to the General Officer Commanding the Orkney and Shetland Defence Force. The man had the cheek to ask me what I was doing in the Orkney Isles! Considering his position, I should have been asking him what on earth I was doing in the Orkney Isles. After about six weeks I came to the conclusion that the answer was – absolutely nothing. One Sunday shortly afterwards I went to church and unwittingly placed myself in the very seat which was apparently reserved each week for Admiral Harwood. One of his anxious aides managed to remove me in the nick of time so I was just spared a confrontation with the victor of the Plate, and further bizarre questions.

My only theatrical activity was to play the part of the Dictator in 'Judgement Day', produced by our Adjutant with the assistance of three young professional actresses of his acquaintance. The part of the seductive spy was undertaken by a certain rather plump and very young Jose Jacques – well-known later as Hattie Jacques.

Marnie Battersby, whom I had met on my way back from the Isle of Man, and I were married at St. Kentigern's Roman Catholic Church in her home town of Blackpool, on the nineteenth of October 1942. Her sister, known to all and sundry then and today as Mopp, was her bridesmaid.

I moved around the U.K. from places as diverse as the Orkney Isles and Bexhill-on-Sea. It was while I was sitting under a haystack by the side of the River Bann in Northern Ireland one night that I was handed a telegram stating, 'Michael has arrived.' Our eldest son is currently a bank manager living in Bristol with his wife Carolyn and children, Edward, Emily and Harry.

An unusual athletic meeting was held on the Woodcote Cricket Ground in Epsom in July 1942. Jack Crump, who lived in Stoneleigh, was for many years the British Amateur Athletic Board's secretary and Britain's Team Manager. He organised a match between the Navy, Army and Air Force against the Police, Civil Defence and others. I was selected as second string to Sydney Wooderson in the mile event. Not only did Epsom have a triple World Record holder at Woodcote that afternoon but Lord Burghley, of Olympic fame, as President of the meeting, and Harold Abrahams, the famous 1924 100 metres Olympic champion (best known today, I expect, as the star of 'Chariots of Fire'), giving a commentary for the BBC. Such an occasion would merit good television coverage forty years later.

I never played cricket on the Woodcote ground myself, but my father had in the 1920s been a regular medium pace bowler for Epsom Wednesday. Wednesday was early closing and this was very much the tradesmen's team.

Epsom Cricket Club moved to its present premises in the 1870s, although being established as far back as the beginning of the century. The Woodcote ground, known as the Schnadhorst Memorial Ground, was purchased by Captain Schnadhorst in 1953. It is a memorial to his father and his son, who was killed in the First World War. I always associated the club with Wilf Walters, whose name I was so often hearing. It appeared, I am told, in a 1922 team, and eventually he was the club's President till 1986. The Surrey Championship Year Book of 1991 records the club's history and continuing success.

Also sharing the Woodcote ground with the Cricket Club and the Tennis Club, under the umbrella of the Epsom Sports Club Ltd., whose Chairman, Arthur Wadsworth, has kindly provided me with information, is the Epsom Hockey Club. The club was conceived at a meeting at the old Epsom Town Hall in 1921 instigated by David Birch, who designed its colours of claret and white halves. As seems to have been the custom with our town's organisations in those days, it was Lord Rosebery who was enrolled as the first President. Men whose names are so familiar to me appear as members – Trower, Cropley, Bowden, Woods and Pullinger.

The Northern Ireland A.A.A. selected me to represent them in the half mile in a match against Eire in Dublin. It was held by some in the 2nd battalion of the Surreys that the only reason for my not being posted abroad was on account of my usefulness in leading the regiment in the News of the World Road Relay Races at Mitcham. We, with considerable help from our Cook Sergeant, Stan Belton a former Surrey champion, won in a field of about a hundred teams on two occasions, beating the course record on one of them.

Eventually some clerk at the 'war house' stuck a pin in my name and I was posted to the Middle East. I said goodbye to the family that now included our second son, Peter – today a Dairy Farm Manager near Newdigate with his wife, Mary, and children David, Paul and Alice – just six hours after Prime Minister Attlee's announcement of the end of the war. Impeccable timing!

We wondered, as we sailed the calm blue Mediterranean in August 1945 under a cloudless sky and watched the red flames above Etna at night, why the ship was so empty. The surprising answer was supplied when we put into Taranto and began to take on board an unbelievable company of eight hundred oddly assorted Jews, who not so long before had been the poor victims of Belsen concentration camp. They made a strange sight in a mixture of prison and other make-do garments – men, women and children. Their emotional singing on deck that evening under the flag of the Star of David was something never to be forgotten. After Haifa the ship was thoroughly disinfected.

Following a brief stay on the Bitter lake, I found myself in the more sophisticated setting of Cairo. I was fortunate enough to spend a couple of afternoons at the Cairo Museum, viewing, amongst other things, the famous Tutankhamen treasures absolutely free and in peace. To stand all alone atop the Great Pyramid was a wonderful experience.

Five months on the staff of the P.T. School at the Middle East Training Centre near Gaza in Palestine followed and the war being ended a rather free-and-easy atmosphere prevailed. This permitted four interesting visits to Jerusalem. My guide on the initial occasion was a young Jewish girl clad in soldier-like khaki, who had a well taught line in propaganda on the subject of 'years of Arab misrule' – as indeed had various pamphlets distributed to service personnel at that time. The state of Israel was not to come into being for three more years. I also spent a week in a very peaceful place called Beirut and a day in Bethlehem, which I was sorry to find more scruffy than sacred. I then concluded my inglorious military career with some grandiosity as 'Acting Commanding Officer of the Middle East School of Physical Training' – which had, in fact, all but ceased to function! Spring flowers now prettily popped up through the sand and I returned to Epsom.

Father had been going through a worrying time. Not only had his manager and chief assistant for some twenty years, Lindsay Hart, left him but my mother had sadly suffered a bad breakdown and had been in various homes for much of that time. He retired to his little bungalow home near Porthscatho in Gerrans Bay, South Cornwall, immediately. I, therefore, came from a rather carefree life under the Palestinian sun to assume the responsibilities of a family and a business – both for the first time. Brother Bob and I coped as best we could with the coal trade under the most adverse of conditions. Marnie and I began our life at 'Three Firs' with our two little sons and food and fuel rationing, but the war was over and we were all safe – we had been lucky.

Epsom as a whole had been lucky too. The bomb damage had been comparatively light. Ashley Court was the worst hit. It so happens that the house where I now live in St. Martins Avenue is a rebuilding of the original 'Beech Tree Cottage', destroyed by a land mine. It was, I am told, the 'doodle bugs' near the war's end that had the worst effect on local morale. Epsom was on their route to London. Air Raid Precautions – later Civil Defence – Home Guard, Fire Watching, Citizens

Advice Bureau (in Waterloo Road), all came into being and played their part. A huge air raid shelter was dug just off Ashley Road – on the right hand side where the hill begins. To this Londoners would come with their blankets and their provisions at night time during the 'blitz' period. Areas within the shelter were allotted names of London streets. The entrance can still be seen among the trees. The Metropolitan Police took over University Motors in Church Street with their black Wolseleys and the Mounted Police the stables on the Downs. But many a town suffered more than we did.

Family history is an easier subject to study if one's family has resided in the same place for a long time. I had always taken some interest in my ancestors in Epsom, but it was not till the spring of 1945, those last few exciting weeks before VE Day, that I actually got down to studying records, making lists and forming some sort of family tree. This may sound a strange time for such a task. The fact was my father was by now becoming depressed by business worries and distressed at my mother's inability to respond to any sort of treatment for her mental illness. He applied for me to be granted compassionate leave for a spell. Bob, who was in the RAF, had been for some time in the unusual position of being stationed in a neutral country – Turkey – and would not be available. Marnie, who had been an Auxiliary Nurse at Horton at the time of our marriage, was now living with her parents in Blackpool, so I was at a loose end some of the time back in Epsom. I went to St. Martin's Church and there began to delve into parish records.

# *Chapter Five*

My investigations at St. Martin's revealed the John Furniss with whom I had hoped to start. In fact there appeared to be a John and a Jonas. They, or he if this could be one and the same person, had a number of children. Elizabeth, born in 1716, was the eldest and this was the earliest date I could find at that time. She was followed by John in 1718, Benjamin 1725, Ann 1728 and in 1736 the twins, Thomas and William. Rebekah followed in 1737 and lastly William (the first William had died in 1736) in 1739. Two of these, Benjamin and William, were to provide some useful little pieces of information for my Epsom history.

It was to be some thirty five years, however, before I was persuaded by a cousin, Fred Baylis (of whose existence I was ignorant till 1980, but who had made a much better study of genealogy than I had), that indeed the John and the Jonas should be presumed as one. It was in the early 1980s, therefore, that I was able with his expert assistance to establish a family tree and even fill in dates prior to 1716. I will reach that point in due course, but in the meantime concentrate on John, Benjamin and William and the Epsom of the eighteenth century.

John Furniss was born in Ewell in 1684. The earliest recorded date of his living in Epsom is the 23rd of March 1716 (according to F. L. Clark) in what was then known as the Common Fields on the south side of the main street. This would, I think, be approximately to the rear of what is now Lester Bowden's in the Ashley Centre. The name occurs as Furnace, Furnass and also as Furnice about that time. John was a carpenter by trade and married to Sarah. He was elected Constable for Epsom on the 15th of October 1719. On the 17th of October 1720 he presented his first annual report which stated 'nil return'. I do not know whether this implies extraordinary good behaviour on the part of the inhabitants or complete lack of effort on my predecessor's part. He would have been well acquainted with the old Watch House in the middle of the street and also the stocks. Pownall, writing in 1825, says the Watch House was in a very poor state, as indeed it had been for a hundred years. John died in 1754, having lived in the reigns of Charles the Second, James the Second, William and Mary, Queen Anne, and George the First and Second. His thirty eight years in Epsom coincided with the peak and decline of Epsom Spa.

Before coming to those times of our town's considerable but short-lived importance, mention must be made of the discovery of the waters (Epsom salts) and of the old wells on the common. In 1989 a book entitled 'Epsom Wells',

A deserted Epsom High Street in about 1875.

The late 17th-century New Tavern and Assembly Rooms in about 1920.

Thomas Furniss (in front of shop window) and his West Street building in 1905.

By the cartoonist, The Canon—early 20th-century.

Coal lorries in 1924.

Volunteers parade in the High Street in 1914.

Epsom Operatic Society. "A Country Girl". Epsom Public Hall 1914.

Tom Walls.

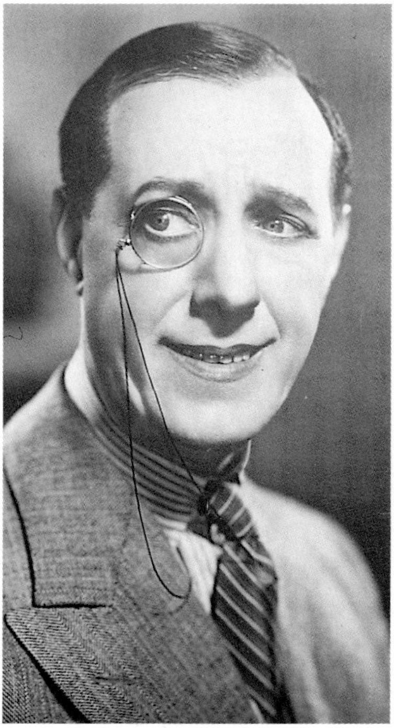

Ralph Lynn.

George and John Furniss. "The Geisha". Ebbisham Hall 1929.

Caricatures of notable Epsomians by The Tout. 1914.

Yew Tree Cottages (Nos. 94–98 High Street). 1920's.

100 High Street and Yew Tree Cottage. 1970's.

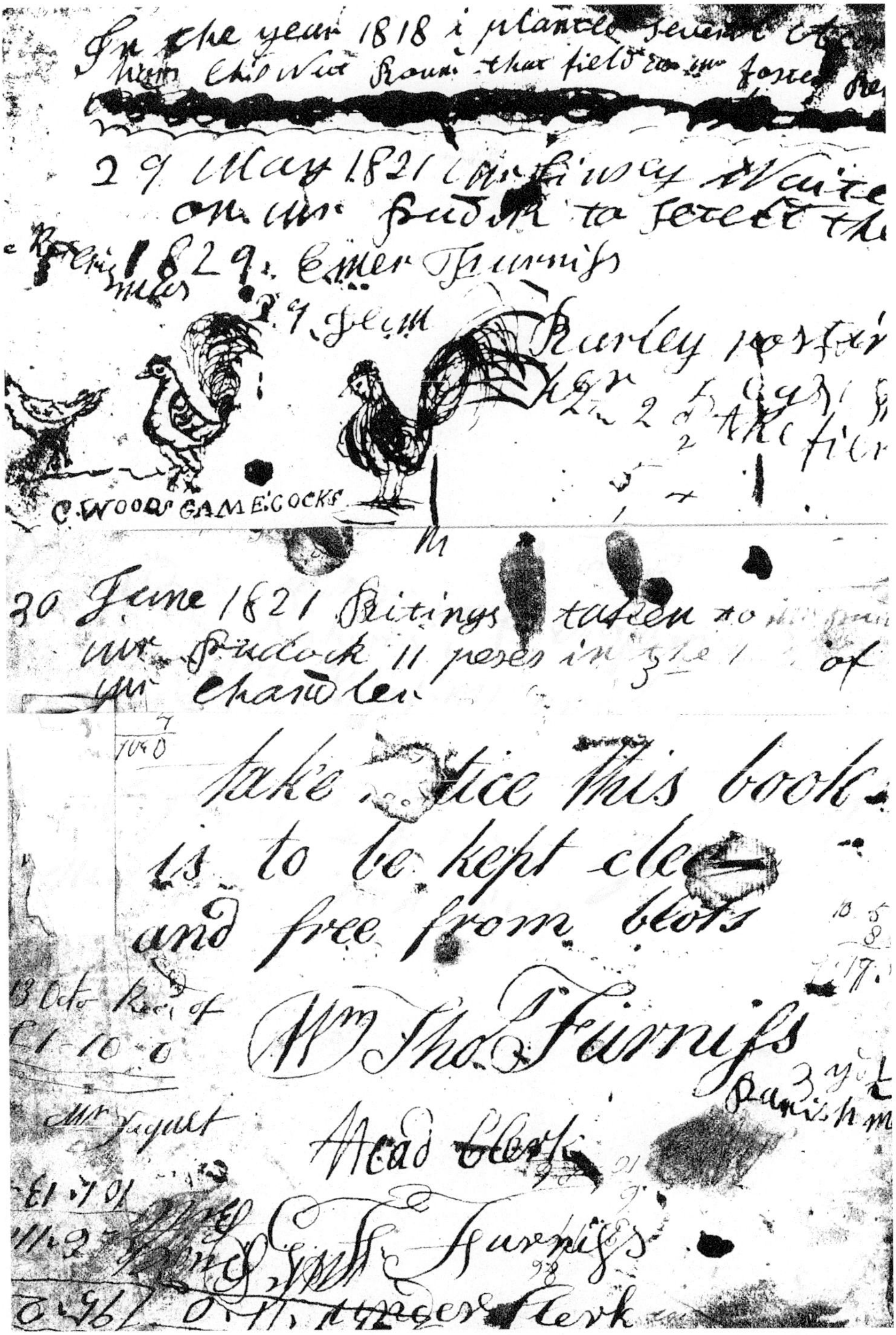


From the old book discovered at 100 High Street in the 1930's, with an instruction from William Thomas Furniss, aged 19.

Epsom Parish Church in 1899—before the alterations of 1907 and the removal of the spire in 1947.

Pitt Place. Demolished 1967.

South Street in 1910.

South Street in 1992.

Derby Day crowds in the High Street 1903.

The Saturday market in 1984.

The King's Head. Demolished 1957.

The Goods Yard in Upper High Street in the 1960's.

The Durdans.

Lord Rosebery.

Late 17th-century Old Vicarage and Cedars Cottage in Church Street.

Before the demolition of the Odeon and adjacent shops. Early 1970's.

A view of old and new Epsom from Sainsbury's car park. 1989.

Tom Walls with his 1932 Derby Winner April the Fifth.

Famous athletes—Sydney Wooderson, Lord Burghley and Harold Abrahams at Woodcote Cricket Ground. 1942.

written by Maurice Exwood, was published by the Borough Council. Therein are some forty pages on the subject and anyone wishing to study the historical and technical details, as most recently researched by Dr. H. L. Lehman and others, will find much of interest well presented.

The story of Henry Wicker in 1618 finding that his cows refused to drink the water from a certain pool on the common – because, as was later discovered, it had an off-putting mineral taste to it – may be more folklore than fact, but it makes a nice story. The waters and their beneficial effects must have been known earlier if by 1629 their fame had spread far and wide. They were already being taken internally as a purgative and not simply externally for the treatment of sores and such like as originally. One wonders how many tummy aches were suffered by those who experimented in this.

By the time Samuel Pepys came on the scene on the 24th of July 1663 Epsom had become quite a famous place. The well was provided with places for shelter, for refreshment and even for entertainment, and was by then visited by thousands of people – the gentry and foreigners. Pepys was surprised to see so many in the town.

'Then rode through Epsom the whole town over, seeing the various companys that were there walking; which was very pleasant to see how they are there, without knowing what to do, but only in the morning to take the waters. But Lord! to see how many I met there of citizens, that I could not have thought to have seen there, that they had ever had it in their heads or purses to go down thither.'

Almost four years later, on the fourteen of July 1667, Pepys again writes of Epsom, where he arrived at eight o'clock in the morning and proceeded straight to the well, having risen to make ready for his coach journey before four o'clock.

He writes that at the well his friends did not partake of the waters 'but I did drink four pints.' On their way to the town they met a poor woman with her pails of milk and 'in one of my gilt tumblers' they drank 'their bellyfull of milk.' At the King's Head he had 'a dish of creame, but it was sour so took no pleasure in it.' After all of that it seems surprising it was his foot that he says Mrs. Turner had to keep her warm hand upon to ease his pain on the return journey!

The King's Head was the town's principal Inn and survived till 1957, being replaced by the King's Shades Walk, now incorporated into the Ashley Centre. Pepys says, ' – to the King's Head and hear that my Lord Buckhurst and Nelly are lodged at the next house, and Sir Charles Sedley with them; and they keep a merry house.'

So we know that colourful seventeenth century character, Nell Gwynne, stayed in our Epsom High Street; though it was not at the house today called Nell Gwynne's House, which in fact did not exist in 1667. The 'merry' house would most likely have been Bramshott House, currently occupied by the Leeds Permanent Building Society and the K Shoe Shop, where she lodged. The poor girl of Drury Lane, who became so popular an actress, excelling in comedy parts, and later to become the King's mistress, did not come to Epsom solely on that July day. She was a frequent visitor, staying in the town for long spells on occasions.

The King had made her a present of stabling at a farm in the old village; that is, in what we now call Church Street. Only very recently has the Farm Garage on that site been replaced by new office buildings – Charles Stuart House and King's Lodge. These are nicely re-created in Stuart period style and are generally agreed to be most welcome, considering what so easily might have been. I think a certain other Charles would approve. Our Nell tired of Epsom in time, perhaps because of her quarrel with Buckhurst, and acquired stables at New-market.

The Ye Old King's Head pub still stands next door to serve twentieth century Epsomians; myself often among them for a lunchtime Guinness – though not at the three old pence per pint I have seen quoted in a mid-nineteenth century local advertisement.

Before I was very old I had learnt of Dr. Livingstone – 'the wicked apothecary' – whom I was led to believe got Epsom a bad name by selling spurious waters in the town, pretending them to be the real thing from the wells on the common. This story came down to me from Pownall, Swete and others via the family. By the time I was beginning to take some interest in our town's history and had re-read F. L. Clark's book 'The History of Epsom Spa' (1960), I began to realise that it was Dr. Livingstone's entrepreneurial zeal and zest that, in fact, more likely created the famous spa in the town, far from destroying it.

The new well in the town, close to today's Magpie public house in South Street, and owned by a Mr. Symonds about the turn of the century, was the basis of what we might today term a 'leisure complex'. The site was approximately from the Magpie to the corner of West Street and back from the road to the present Manor House Court on the higher level. The rather higgledy-piggledy mess we see today, of back doors, back yards, alleys, new buildings, and cars awaiting repair, was, in the years following 1707, Epsom Spa.

As master-minded by Livingstone, it was destined to become a popular attraction, not only for the gentry and the aristocracy but even for royalty; not only for the English pleasure seekers of fashion but for distinguished foreigners from many parts of Europe. Prince George of Denmark, Consort of Queen Anne, was a regular visitor.

'Where fashion resolve, To raise Epsom to fame, Poor Tunbridge Wells did nought.' Temporarily Epsom exceeded Bath, it was said. (This is extremely unlikely and probably the result of some good P.R. work.). Livingstone's Spa boasted coffee houses, shops for hats, shoes, ribbons, books, and sweetmeats; and groves with delightful arbours, two bowling greens, breakfast music, evening music, dancing and, of course, there was the New Tavern with its various attractions too.

'The post will go every day to and fro betwixt London and Epsom during the season for taking the waters,' an advertisement stated.

Much of the structure and indeed interesting parts of the interiors of the shops on the site (including the Albion public house, formerly 'The Coffee House') nearly three hundred years later are still there. The Albion's first floor room was used in the last century as the Magistrate's Court. The present decoration on the front of the building is only Victorian and later than 1860. The fronts of these buildings are so altered, with additions and repairs and with new shop windows and modern advertising, that Epsomians now pass by without a thought of what fashionable elegance and colourful amusement once existed there.

Celia Fiennes, writing at the time, seems to be impressed by the trees and the way they were looked after. John Toland in 1726 says, 'I must needs say that even the houses of the townsmen are everywhere mighty neat. The fronts adorned with rows of elm and lime trees, close enough to defend those who sit under such hospitable shades from the injuries of the sun and rain. Here sometimes breakfast and supper are taken, as at other times a cheerful glass and a pipe.' I like to imagine he was writing of the Yew Tree Cottages.

By 1740 fashion changed and the 'quality' had almost deserted Epsom, finding new places of amusement. Epsom was perhaps a little too close to London. Its fame dwindled and it returned to being the poorer and quieter place it had been earlier. Livingstone died in 1727.

In 1754 an advertisement for Epsom old well ended 'The Purging Waters of this place are in excellent order.' This was somewhat optimistic, and Lord Rosebery in his introduction to Gordon Home's book calls it 'pathetic'.

For many years, till very recently, the old well site on the Wells Estate on Epsom Common was marked by a small pedestal surrounded by railings. In 1989 the Borough Council greatly improved the area, which had become somewhat run down, and a little ceremony was held on June the twenty-fifth.

o 0 o

The famous name of Epsom may also be found upon a map of Indiana in the United States. It seems that in the tiny hamlet of Tophet – possibly a nickname taken from the Bible and meaning a place for the refuse of Jerusalem and in time becoming synonymous with Hell – a well was dug early in the nineteenth century which was found to produce water with a mineral flavour very like Epsom Salts. The good folk of Tophet quickly discarded their unflattering name for that of

Epsom. The new Epsom thrived and had a schoolroom built of logs by 1846 and a post office by 1856.

Very recently I was fortunate enough, thanks to the insistence of my cousin, Elliott Stephenson ('Steve'), who lives in Arizona, to make an extensive car tour of the U.S.A., and with some difficulty we found Epsom. A young woman, wearing the traditional white bonnet of the Menonite folk, in answer to my question 'Can you please direct me to Epsom?', pointed to a tiny Methodist church, a handful of little white houses, a few barns, some chickens and pigs. 'This is it' she said. The total population she reckoned to be about forty or fifty. For any information about the old days she directed us to Chester Stanley, who 'has been here since ever'. It appeared Epsom no longer possesses a Post Office, a school nor even a shop. It seemed lost miles from anywhere on a track through the fields. The old man told us he once ran the village store, and pointed to a pathetic derelict wooden building by the side of the dusty road.

I obtained the original information from a remarkable nonagenarian, Arthur Mussett by name, whose son lives in America. Arthur was a popular and much respected member of the staff of Long Grove Hospital for nearly fifty years, where he built up and controlled the laboratory.

o 0 o

By the time John Furniss arrived in Epsom from Ewell in 1716 the Spa had already been well established. He came to a busy place. When he died in 1754 it had all changed. Of his second and fifth sons, Benjamin and William, I have gleaned some information to contribute to my Epsom story in the middle part of the eighteenth century and will firstly deal with Benjamin, who was born in 1725. He was a tailor by trade, who worked and lived close by the King's Head. He married Susannah Brown of Epsom and had three children. He was a Churchwarden at St. Martin's and was also a member of a Masonic Lodge meeting at the Spread Eagle.

The year my Uncle Tom died (1928), he wrote a letter to his younger brother, part of which I quote: 'Dear Geo. Re. old Ben. Ben at the latter part of his life formed the habit of walking over to "The Haunch of Venison" (now Forest Lodge) every afternoon, and on one occasion promised to be over as usual next day for some particular function. He, however, was otherwise engaged and was buried on March 25th, 1798, aged 74. His grave is next to the wall in line with grandfather's. It has the quotation "Boast not thyself of tomorrow for thou knowest not what a day may bring forth" – and that's all I know about he.'

The writer himself died shortly after penning this letter, and I know my father was deeply upset at the loss of his only brother at the age of fifty-six. Uncle Tom had retired to Salcombe in South Devon only a few years earlier. I have found the Haunch of Venison on an old map and indeed it was on the right by that curve in the road between Epsom and Ashtead. Strangely, this vanished pub is a link between Benjamin and William Furniss, who was born in 1739.

William was a coachman. He is mentioned in local records dated 1761. This was a hazardous occupation, apart from any other reason, on account of the exposure to the elements, and by all accounts the winters of his time tended to be most severe. One bitterly cold day in 1776, returning from I know not where, he was taken ill by the time his coach had reached Ashtead. He could go no further than the Haunch of Venison, where he was carried in and tended by the landlord and his wife. But the extreme cold had beaten him and there he died. He left a wife, Jane (Stuart), three daughters and two sons. The elder, three years old at the time of his father's untimely death at the age of only thirty-seven, was the Thomas who became the tailor at Yew Tree Cottage – the great great grandfather of whom I have already written.

Whilst the spa was in decline, and Benjamin and William were still young, there came upon the scene, according to Pownall and retold by Swete, an unusual character called 'Crazy Sally'. 1736 seems to be the date of the beginning of Sally Wallin's operations in the town, when she showed her genius at mending broken bones and resetting disjointed limbs. When she tried to leave Epsom to marry a certain Mr. Mapp, the inhabitants did all they could to prevent her from going, and she is supposed to have refused to correct a dislocated neck till she was freed.

I always liked the story of how she dealt with certain surgeons who had refused to acknowledge her. They presented her with an imposter to be cured. Sally quickly broke the unfortunate man's limbs, re-directing him to the surgeons who had sent him. When I was suffering for some years from what was popularly known as 'slipped disc', I seem to remember some divergence of views between doctors and osteopaths.

o 0 o

Nobody who had to cope with the immediate post-war conditions in the extraordinary winter of 1946–7 is likely to forget it. It was the hardest in living memory and none has been quite so severe since. 1962–63 was bad, but not like that.

As coal merchants, Bob and I were responsible not only for trying to see all our customers had their fair share of what was in very short supply, but record all supplies to 'registered' customers, keeping their deliveries within the prescribed ration of 34 cwts of house coal and 40 cwts of boiler fuel per year. This, of course, meant keeping a credit account even for those who were really 'cash customers', taking only very small deliveries. In addition there were 'supplementary certificates' in the case of illness or special hardship, issued by the Local Fuel Officer, to contend with. For emergencies, we had to transport coal from the goods yard to the rear of our shop, making a large dump from which people could collect their own supplies. We had queues of cars, wheelbarrows and even prams at the peak of the bad weather. What people never seemed to understand was that in really terrible conditions of snow and ice the ability to fill frozen sacks, carry coal on one's back, start petrol engines and drive big lorries on slippery roads is in inverse proportion to the needs of shivering people, invalids, babies and the aged, to have the warmth that in those days only solid fuel could provide.

My brother Bob was in charge of the coal yard and the deliveries side of the business, and I recall his desperation some early mornings in the half light, when the coalmen could not even prize open their frozen sacks, despite lighting bonfires. Both of us had to use our cars to convey fuel in small sacks, bags or boxes, utilising the back seat and the boot. The office staff were inundated with phone calls. So called 'urgent lists' were so long that in time we had 'urgent urgents' till they just had to be abandoned altogether.

The wintry weather persisted all through January and February till March. I remember icicles instead of blossom on the trees. The Reigate Road was blocked for some weeks by the east wind sweeping across Priesthill fields opposite and forming drifts deeper than any since the famous snowstorm that began on Boxing Day 1927. That season the snow created drifts over twelve feet high. We were cut off and sledges had to be used to bring food up from Ewell Village. In 1947, at least, the road did not take so long to clear.

Fuel shortages were not confined to 1946 and 47. The problem continued well into the 1950s and each winter presented the same situation – at least to some extent.

Sad to say, Mother died in 1946. On a happier note our son Tim was born in 1948 and at the end of 1949 Martin arrived, to complete our quartet of boys. Today they both live in Devon. Tim is a free lance journalist. For some years now he has concentrated on the subject of Space and has to his credit many books, broadcasts and TV appearances. He and Sue have two children, Tom and Katie. Martin recently decided to train as a teacher, at Plymouth and is married to Sarah, with children Christopher, Simeon and Sadie Kate. Marnie obviously spent many a year pushing prams and coping with the energetic quartet – I may say without the fridge, freezer, dishwasher, washing machine, second car and such like, as many young wives would expect today.

In time Father married Marjorie Morris and they lived in the little bungalow in Cornwall's Roseland, with a wonderful view of the sea and of Porthscatho. Bob, who was with us at 'Three Firs' for a time, then married Corinne and with two sons, Stephen and Geoffrey, born in 1951 and 1955 respectively, continues to live in Epsom. By 1950 we had a half-sister, Evelyn, now Mrs. Dean and living near Swindon.

Four years later, one July evening, I received a telephone call from Marjorie: Dad had died from a heart attack. He had been up to Epsom but occasionally and I to Cornwall only about four times in recent years, so I was not so close to him in the end as I had been at work and play in those youthful pre-war days, which somehow one felt would last for ever. In 1954 he was not yet quite seventy.

o 0 o

By 1946 I had been a Blackheath Harrier for thirteen years. It now seemed to me I should also be an Epsom Harrier. I was pleased to be accepted as such and meet that tireless worker and great enthusiast, George Tolley, the club's secretary, and to meet new friends.

By August I found myself in a happy party of athletes from Epsom and Ewell; young women as well as men, on my way to Holland to compete with the local club at Hilversum. It was a wonderful experience to meet those hospitable Dutch people so soon after the end of the war. I returned in 1949, and in the meantime had acted as one of the hosts when the Gooise Athletick Club came to Epsom. It is good to be able to report that these excellent exchanges continue into the 1990s.

Epsom Harriers was founded in 1890. Lord Rosebery was its first President and the club continues to wear his rose and primrose colours. In the mid-1930s there were some fifty members. Today there are seven times that number. Another notable official in the realm of British athletics, apart from George Tolley, who also lived in Stoneleigh, was Jack Crump. He was the secretary of the British Amateur Athletics Board from the 1930s to 50s and was the British Team manager for a number of years, including 1948 when Britain hosted the Olympic Games. Observing the signs of a kind of professionalism creeping in, even then, I well recall his words, 'They are spoiling our sport, John.' One of the two starters at Wembley was Harry Grindall, who lived in Epsom's Copse Edge Avenue.

Although my event had previously been the half mile, from 1946 onwards I concentrated on the Steeplechase and, largely on account of taking second place in the Southern Counties Two Miles Steeplechase at Motspur Park in 1947, no doubt, became what was known as an 'Olympic possible'. People today would be surprised to learn that this qualified me for food parcels from Australia, such was the situation in Britain in those immediate post-war years. I was only too well aware that, in reality, I must be regarded as an 'Olympic improbable'. Four Epsom and Ewell Harriers, Ron Ede, Margaret Birtwhistle, Kaye Long and Elspeth White, were, however, in the eventual team at Wembley Stadium that exceptionally humid and thundery week. I was a more-than-interested spectator on five of the athletics afternoons; something I repeated twelve years later when the Olympic Games were held in Rome.

That memorable car trip in 1960, of some three thousand miles in all, was to be the first of many family holidays touring in France, Italy, Germany, Switzerland, Austria and Yugo-Slavia. We were introduced to the wonderful carefree pleasures of camping by our good friends, James and Gwenda Ryan of Ashley Road, and have every reason to be grateful to them ever since. As the years have gone by the children, one by one, have naturally gone their own ways, but Marnie and I still enjoy the same kind of summer activity – nine cars and three tents later.

The Harriers continue to score their successes, both in cross country and on the track. From 1964 they used the, then new, cinder track at the Poole Road Recreation Ground, but this has now deteriorated too badly and the members regretfully have to train outside the Borough. I observe, as I travel around on our annual tours, that communities of Epsom's size, or even smaller, in other countries usually possess modern all-weather plastic tracks. It is not only in Epsom and Ewell but in Britain as a whole that we are somewhat behind the times in the provision of up-to-date sports facilities.

o 0 o

It was in 1949 that, after almost exactly ten years, the Ebbisham Hall was again available for public performances. That old favourite, 'The Desert Song', was the chosen vehicle for the Epsom Operatic Society's resumption after the long interval of war. I found myself acting as producer, in Father's absence in Cornwall till the final weeks, and much relished the task.

George Furniss had unquestionably been the district's leading theatrical personality and most popular provider of local entertainment for close on half a century. He now retired. From then onwards I produced sixteen of the Society's twenty three musicals up to 1970.

'The Desert Song' was greeted each night with overwhelming applause and even cheers. This was not due, I have to say, to any exceptional artistic achievement on our part but was Epsom's spontaneous expression of relief and happiness that the war was over and things were back to normal.

I played the main comedy part and was delighted, as well as surprised, to find people actually laughed.

In 1952 I was fortunate enough to meet Felton Rapley, who was then living in Hookfield before moving to Alexandra Road. He had been cinema organist for Gaumont British for some years, a frequent performer at the BBC Theatre Organ, conductor of many shows in the London area and was the staff arranger for the well-known music firm, Chappell's. As well as acting as Musical Director for nine of my productions over the next twelve years, he was also organist and choirmaster at St. Martin's Church, where his characteristic playing – a little on the loud side and a little on the fast side – was always exciting. Felton was a Gilbert & Sullivan expert and consequently a marvellous guide when I first undertook those operas in 1957. Eventually in retirement in Winchester, he was often pressed to act as rehearsal pianist for the local Gilbert & Sullivan company, and I know what a great thrill it was for him, at the end of his days, to stand in for the organist at Winchester's great cathedral.

Four local amateurs who performed with me in Epsom have become successful professionals. David Ryall was a National Theatre actor under Olivier and is still appearing on our television screens. Frank Egerton has been one of Covent Garden's regular tenors for some twenty years and is now internationally known. Marilyn Hill Smith, who had the tiniest part in my 'Oklahoma', is today much in demand, particularly in operetta, both at our opera houses and on the concert platform. Nicholas Smith (from Downs Avenue at the time) will probably be best remembered as the harassed Manager in television's 'Are You Being Served?'

It was P. G. Wodehouse who said it was just when a chap was feeling particularly braced with himself that fate sneaked up behind him with a piece of lead piping. I had been a producer for three years or so and was feeling, I must admit, 'braced with myself'. I occasionally had to purchase various small items for the productions on the Epsom Society's behalf. The Treasurer, instead of putting these under the appropriate headings on the annual accounts, had placed them all in total under my name. At the Annual General Meeting one of the most prominent members rose: 'Mr. Chairman,' he solemnly and pompously began, 'if we are to pay John £26, would it not be better to engage a professional and have a proper producer?' On the subject of things that might have been put differently, I will go back to 1906. Lindsay Harman, of the D'Oyly Carte Company, had been engaged to produce 'HMS Pinafore' at Leatherhead and was having trouble with the ladies' chorus in the ensemble with the men, 'Sailors always welcome ladies most politely'. They had to curtsey at the end of the number on the first syllable of the word 'politely'. After they had got it all wrong a number of times, the exasperated Mr. Harman said firmly, 'Ladies, ladies, I want to see you all bob down on the po.'

Belonging to about the same period comes the following from the gentleman in 'The Gondoliers' playing the part of Giuseppe to the gentleman playing Marco: 'You know, the trouble with you is you think too much of yourself; you are too big-headed. You should just play the part and forget yourself like I do. That's what makes me so good.'

The 1950s provided a new experience for me. I was asked to produce for the Tudor Players, a company based in the Twickenham area, and spent an exciting week at the Kingston Empire with 'Magyar Melody'. The dancers all came with me from Epsom as the Ebbisham Dancers. Unfortunately, the regular Empire public, used to their weekly variety bill, stayed away. The play's author, Eric Maschwitz, whom I got to know well later, joked – 'One week of John Furniss and they turn the Empire into a supermarket.' It still is. I later produced operas – my first in that particular field – at Twickenham, and the same decade provided the opportunity to appear at both the Scala Theatre (now demolished) and the Fortune Theatre (by the side of Drury Lane). After these two performances with the Coal Trade Dramatic Society, I was asked to produce for them at the Scala – my one and only 'straight' play production.

Jan Poore, still resident in Epsom, became, for some years after 1970, the one chiefly responsible for the E.A.O. & D.S. plays, and it was during this period that the name was changed to the present Epsom Players. Somewhat later, under the leadership of Norma and Peter Evans, the Epsom Light Opera Society undertook more of the comic opera and operetta field.

Elsie Green, who lives near me in St. Martin's Avenue, achieved a considerable reputation as organiser and director of the annual open-air plays at Polesdon Lacey. She was the person largely responsible for bringing Shakespeare to local audiences – both at Polesdon Lacey and at the Ebbisham Hall. She also performed a notable service as a speech therapist and was awarded the OBE a few years ago. I was lucky to be associated with her in one of her Shakespeare productions. Elsie, despite her age, is still involved in the world of drama.

# *Chapter Six*

Moving house is said to be one of life's most traumatic experiences. In 1923 to me it was but a little adventure. In 1957 it took place not only on the Thursday between the Derby and the Oaks, but a bare six weeks before Marnie was expecting our fifth child. Both events (the move and the birth) went off well. We were delighted with our larger house in St. Martin's Avenue and even more so with – at last – a daughter. She is now a District Nurse, recently moved to Malvern, married to Tim Trimble and the mother of William and Christopher. As Catherine went to the Convent of the Sacred Hearts School and later trained and worked at the Epsom District Hospital, she was, by chance, for some nineteen years obliged to spend much of her life in the Dorking Road.

I well recall the grim old Workhouse on the site of the present hospital. Parts still survive. Here was once the Infirmary – the Isolation or Fever Hospital being in Hook Road. The Horse Pound (now a little plot of grass in front of the hospital) was still there long after the horse era and well into that of the motor car, as I remember.

Just down the road, on the same side by the cricket ground, F. J. Seymour had his Nurseryman's business from 1935. He had begun in the Parade in 1918. It was in 1955 that his sons, Basil and Denis, opened their large Garden Centre on the Ewell By-Pass – with Horticulture on the Reigate Road, and subsequently Landscape and Leisure on the Cheam Road based at Pit House. Since 1740 Pit House had previously been an inn, a private house and a library.

As a magistrate, Basil Seymour served on the bench in Epsom for twenty two years, including a record nine years as its Chairman.

Our church, St. Joseph's in Heathcote Road, whose Parish Priest was an old character by name Canon Christall, was quite close to our new home. The longest serving Parish Priests in my time have been – Father Chatterton, Monseigneur Westlake and Father Heaney. Next door was, conveniently, our 'local', The Rising Sun, run by the popular Cecil Stacey.

Epsom's Parish Church of St. Martin's was, in fact, even closer to us and, as with many parish churches, merits the recording of some historical information. With one's back to Ye Olde King's Head, one now sees a large forecourt and a wide flight of steps leading to the west front of the church. This has, however, only been the case since 1922. When I was a little boy, living in Worple Road, Pagden's Brewery stood in front of the tower and extended nearly half way across the frontage, presenting a very different aspect. When part of the brewery was demolished, the remainder was rebuilt in seventeenth century style to create the present Church House. Another major change in my time, and as recently as 1947, was the removal of the tall spire from the tower for reasons of safety.

o 0 o

Now to go back to the beginnings. The Domesday Book records Epsom (Ebesham) as possessing two churches; one presumably a Saxon church on the present site, and the other possibly in Woodcote. The list of Rectors and Vicars at the church door shows the first as being in 1273. On that same day that Samuel Pepys rose at four o'clock, and with a supply of wine and beer arrived at Epsom Well by eight – the fourteenth of July 1667 – he tells us he walked from the King's Head to the church (via the Parade no doubt) and found a surprisingly small congregation, but that 'Mr. Evelyn and his lady, and also my Lord George Berkeley's lady and their fine daughter, that the King of France liked so well and did dance so rich in jewells before the King at the ball I was at, at our Court last winter, and also their son, a Knight of the Bath, were at church this morning.' Richard Evelyn lived at Woodcote Park and was the brother of the diarist, John Evelyn. The church was by then the mid-fifteenth century rebuilding.

In 1823 a committee was formed to discuss the building of a new church. Serving on this were: Sir James Alexander, who lived at The Clock House (still standing) in Dorking Road and was one of the town's most influential men of the day; James Trotter, whose name I have noted in great great grandfather's old account book; Henry Pownall, the author of the 1825 book on Epsom; and Mr. Jaquet, the previously mentioned Postmaster. It was planned to build a church to accommodate eleven hundred people. The architect, Charles Hatchard, designed a new church with a facing of broken flints, similar in style to the old one and, as the existing tower was considered strong enough, this was incorporated as the dominant feature in the new building. Today, therefore, we still possess a mediaeval tower and octagonal turret at the north west corner, after almost five hundred and fifty years. The bells, I am pleased to say, still ring out so pleasantly on Sundays and for special occasions. A sum of £6,000 was agreed and in 1824 the new church completed. Gordon Home mentions in his 1901 book that a later critic referred to the building as being a 'pseudo-Gothic structure of the commonest type.'

In 1907 there was a plan to demolish and create a new and larger church. However, owing to lack of money, a compromise had to be found and the church was enlarged by what amounts to an extension at the eastern end. The result has never been considered satisfactory, being a partial demolition of the 1824 building and partial erection of the proposed plan. In the churchyard is a memorial to all those whose graves were disturbed in 1907.

There is also the family tomb of the Northeys and that of Arthur Heathcote. Inside, a certain John Braithwaite, who died in 1800, inspired the most lengthy and 'over-the-top' eulogy imaginable. References to benevolence, rectitude, righteousness, moderation and every possible virtue are scattered with abandon over the marble. Such words as religious, moral, affectionate, sincere, generous, just, beloved, respected, revered, loved and honoured appear. It ends, 'Assured of blessed immortality.' He should be.

Nearby is a memorial to John Parkhurst, Lord of the Manor, who created considerable improvements at the Old Wells on the common in the 1690s.

There is also a tablet to the memory of great grandfather William Thomas Furniss, who was the Parish Clerk for many years. He died in 1874. Eighty years later a memorial service was held in the church in the presence of some two hundred people for his grandson – my father.

Anthony Howard, sometimes seen on television as a political commentator, is the son of a former vicar.

St. Barnabas' Church in Hook Road, whose Priest, Michael Godwin, I was pleased to know, was originally a small corrugated iron building. I dimly recall the wedding of my cousin, Margery, to Edgar Bradley, who was the church's organist. A photograph tells me that was in my Eton collar days and was at the present church, with the frontage in Temple Road.

Sandwiched in between East Street and the Victoria railway line, and hardly noticed today, is a much older church – the tiny disused Presbyterian chapel dating back to the 1700's. This is in Prospect Place, which can be approached from Church Road or from Clayton Road, off East Street opposite the Plough and Harrow public house, where a few interesting old cottages survive. In the chapel's little graveyard is the tombstone of the wife of George Snashall, whose shop was in the High Street by the Wellington. My mother was, I remember, a regular customer, and as a small child my toys would have come from there, if not from Chambers on the other side of the road and in, what we used to call, 'the narrow end'.

The shift of Epsom from being a little cluster around the church to the more spacious present day centre around the Watch House and the pond did not, of course, take place overnight. It may have commenced at the end of Tudor times, but certainly during the first half of the seventeenth century. Today's Epsom is basically Stuart, even if we now regrettably have so little to show for it. Various lime pits created in our Saxon days still exist – half way up Burgh Heath Road, in the Alexandra Road Recreation Ground, near the bottom of Downs Road (now the secluded Elizabeth Welchman Gardens) and right in the old village where flats have replaced Pitt Place.

At the time of the Domesday Book, Ebesham was one of the manors held by the Abbot of Chertsey. Somewhat later the lesser manors of Horton and Brettgrave were formed by sub-division and both names are currently in use. The Domesday Book mentions a mere forty three souls. Women and children did not count. Neither did – as W. S. Gilbert put it – 'clumsy clodhoppers with axes and choppers and people of lowly degree.' In a book by Reginald White he estimates something like three hundred inhabitants. For a period Henry the Eighth held the manor himself and then in time the names of Carew, Darcy, Mynn, Lewknor, Parkhurst and Mawbey appear as Lords of the Manor.

The road, little more than a rough track, through the village, was that from Reigate via Bones Gate to Kingston, and would approximate locally to the present Burgh Heath Road, Church Road and Pikes Hill. A further track connected with Epsom Court near Pound Lane. This last mentioned, and still much used today, was part of the old road from Leatherhead via Craddocks Lane to Ewell – The Portway. Our Dorking Road, East Street and Kingston Road did not exist.

Even up to 1755 it was just not possible to travel by carriage in the winter months, but that year considerable improvements began to be made, including the road to Sutton by Howell Hill and one through the Mickleham Valley from Horsham.

o 0 o

In the late 17th century and during the 18th, a number of rich people who wanted to live in the country, but not too far from London, began to favour the Epsom area, which seemed to offer them many attractions. We are indeed fortunate that, despite the ravaging of the developers' bulldozers over the last thirty years, a number of remarkably fine houses still grace Church Street. When walking there and contemplating these houses today it would be rewarding, if one might find the time, to indulge in the luxury of letting one's thoughts wander into another age, imagining the lives, the manners and the costumes of the Epsom residents who once lived in them; helped maybe by some promptings from Sheridan's 'The School for Scandal' or 'The Rivals', picturing perhaps a coach on the gravel driveway here and a Lady Teazle or a Mrs. Malaprop in the doorway there.

On the right leaving the town is No. 10, Hope Lodge. Regrettably No. 8, Cromwell Lodge, a fine late eighteenth century building, became much neglected and was demolished under controversial circumstances some fifteen years ago. Home says, 'The last old gentleman to give up the bob wig in Epsom was a Mr. Storey who lived at Cromwell Lodge in 1838.'.

On the left, a little further up, is The Hermitage, No. 45, standing back from the road and on a slightly lower level. This is the exception in that it pre-dates all the other houses in the road. It is late Tudor and is, apart from the church tower, the only pre-seventeenth century building still in existence. It is, therefore, the sole representative of our old Epsom village. On the left is Grove Road and left again The Grove and Grove House. This particularly fine white late eighteenth century house is the largest in the area and most impressive, standing well away from the road. On the right of Church Street and on the corner of Worple Road is The Cedars, built about 1690, now housing the Citizens Advice Bureau and the Day Centre. Many Epsomians will remember with pleasure, but also with sadness, the two great and ancient cedar trees which stood outside. The famous storm of October 1987 removed them both. I have recently been told that Mr. Barrett of Wimpole Street, father of Elizabeth, owned the premises for a period.

Next comes the long low Cedars Cottage, No. 16, of the same date, and part of the same premises – recently the residence of Geoffrey Aronson. Each of the historic Church Street houses are surprisingly quite different. At No. 18 we have the well proportioned Old Vicarage, now occupied by a firm of solicitors. This dates from the late 17th century and is of most attractive red brick. Richmond House, though built in the style of the 18th century, is Regency, and a most impressive white building it is. Parkhurst, now Park Place House, No. 24, is unsymmetrical, of three stories and at a right angle to the road, belonging to the late 17th century, but with additions. No. 24, A and B, is the Coach House, again late 17th century, and most probably the site of those Nell Gwynne stables. On the left is Stone House by the church – part 17th century and part modern. It is now divided into Nos. 59 and 59A. Ye Olde King's Head on the right again and facing the church is 17th century and on the same site of a former inn. Ebbisham House, No. 30, has only very recently had its two wings demolished and replaced with much larger ones. The original middle section dates from about 1720. The result of the rebuilding has been to create a huge office block whose size is now somewhat out of proportion and unsympathetic in its surroundings.

We now come to the site of the former Pitt Place opposite. A quite remarkable mid-18th century house once stood in the old chalk pit where there are now rather grim blocks of so-called luxury flats. Gordon Home in his usual fulsome manner provides details – 'literally contained within the circumference of a chalk pit . . . the luxuries of life into the above small compass – a good house, one room 30 feet by 20 feet and 15 feet high. In its gardens (all within the pit) is hot house, greenhouse, orangery, vinery, pinery, a grove, terrace, fish ponds, fountain with rock work, the largest gold and silver fish I ever saw, a hot and cold bath, a pretty shrubbery; in short one cannot name anything that is not in this wonderful chalk pit.' He also makes much of the story of the death in 1779 of Lord Lyttleton after 'a woman appeared to him in white apparel and said to him, "Prepare to die; you will not exist these three days." ' And he did not.

In 1967, despite two Building Preservation Orders, the house was, without warning, demolished over one weekend, causing considerable controversy and much questioning, amounting, as I well recall, to something of a furore – but of course all too late.

When living in the Reigate Road we used to see quite a lot of the Epsom College boys. This school was founded in 1851. The rather sprawling red brick buildings and spacious grounds were opened in 1855 as the Royal Medical Benevolent College. For a time all the boys were sons of doctors.

Years ago we used to admire schoolboys' neat suits, straight ties, short hair and coloured caps. Now suits have all but disappeared and those that survive seem to be accompanied by crooked ties, long hair and no caps. In mid-afternoon schoolgirls may be seen in a variety of dress or undress to stagger along with their clothes and books stuffed into miscellaneous plastic bags.

For a little while in the 1960s I was a frequent visitor to Ewell Technical College – later NESCOT – in an attempt to create the Adrian Mann Theatre Guild there. The theatre was named after the former Councillor (Mayor 1950). A project I relished was conjuring with all the many scenes, costumes, small parts and both live and recorded music in Noel Coward's 'Cavalcade', with Pamela Brown and Yvonne Wallis most notable in the cast.

The Principal of the College was at that time Lt. Col. Buchanan, who happened to be my C.O. for a short while during the war. A year or so later I had occasion to speak to his successor about my problems with the students, and in the mildest of criticisms dared to utter the word 'discipline'. He gasped. 'Don't mention that word here,' he said.

o 0 o

By the time we moved to Beech Tree Cottage I was forty-one. I had been producing amateur shows for eight years, acting in them for twenty-eight and taking at least some interest in matters theatrical for thirty-six. To an amateur like myself professionals were all but gods and goddesses in their own magic world; quite separate people one could only admire from a distance.

By 1957 it was beginning to occur to me that the retail coal trade belonged very much to the Victorian era and the first half of the twentieth century, that the second half was bound to see an accelerating decline; and that it would belong to the next century not at all. Would our little business support both myself and my brother and our families for long enough? I began to have vague, though not particularly serious, thoughts about some alternative. Television was in its infancy. Eric Maschwitz was still showing considerable enthusiasm for my efforts and was well placed to make useful contacts. There would be no harm in asking. Eric had been the Editor of the Radio Times, author of many a musical from 'Balalaika' to 'Love from Judy', was popular and seemed to know everybody. I soon had an invitation to meet him in London and for the next five years had many interesting experiences such as I could never have imagined.

Various interviews with the BBC and ITV companies followed. Some interviewers were vaguely sympathetic, some pretended to be interested, but most were quick to advise me to keep well out of it. Advice from Eric: 'Don't forget they are just as afraid of you as you are of them.' Ronnie Waldman, Head of Light Entertainment, referred me rapidly to the TV Music Department, where I met Kenneth Wright, who was most friendly. For a few months we had many an interesting chat over coffee and BBC chocolate biscuits. Before some heart trouble, Kenneth had been No. 1 but now he was No. 2. Looking back, I think all he really wanted was someone to talk to.

During this period I met (very briefly) a number of well-known performers. One of a most interesting and colourful assortment I actually had a few words with was Petula Clarke, who had been born in West Ewell and attended the Danetree School there. Incidentally the actor Stewart Grainger was also at one time a Ewellian.

The Light Entertainment Department thought I would be 'just the job' for the Music Department, and the Music Department thought I would be 'just the job' for the Light Entertainment Department. In the end, as I should very well have known, I was 'just the job' for nobody.

One exciting spin-off from my friendship with Eric Maschwitz was the opportunity to go back-stage at the Theatre Royal, Drury Lane. To stand on the stage at 'the Lane' had always been one of my father's ambitions, as well as mine, and I am pleased to say he just achieved it before he died. Later I met Bill Abingdon, the theatre's Stage Director, who arranged those wonderfully spectacular effects in the Ivor Novello shows, when, in semi-retirement, he was running the old Grantham's scenery business in Hylands Road, Leatherhead. Another local connection with the famous theatre was through my cousin, Gwen Cracknell (of the Ewell butcher's firm already referred to) who, as Gwen May, had appeared there in two musical shows early in the 1930s. Thanks to the kindness of Frankie Vaughan, I was to be her escort when he arranged a return back-stage visit for her at the age of eighty.

Amongst the people to whom I had written was Douglas Craig, the Assistant General Administrator of Glyndebourne Festival Opera. Surprisingly I got a prompt and positive reply, with an invitation to attend certain rehearsals at that unique Sussex house. As it happened, an Epsom singer who had appeared with me in Epsom Operatic shows, Susan Gray, had just become a professional and was in the Glyndebourne chorus. I therefore had both one of the staff and one of the cast to show me round.

At lunch on my first day I found myself sitting opposite a youngish man in an old blue sweater, who was obviously Welsh. I was informed his name was Geraint Evans. On a visit to the 'gents', where we chaps all meet on equal terms so to speak, I was actually spoken to by Carl Ebert, the famous producer, who had once worked with Max Reinhardt and directed opera in Berlin, which he left in 1933. He was Glyndebourne's Artistic Director for many years. At the conclusion of the dress rehearsal of 'The Magic Flute', with some trepidation (because it was really against the rules) I went on to the stage, approached the Professor, as Ebert was called, and uttered a few words of praise and thanks for what had been a wonderful experience. He replied: 'How sweet of you to say so, dear boy. You must come whenever you wish' ('veneffer you vish' actually), which proves, I suppose, that flattery will get you somewhere.

I was subsequently allowed to watch a performance of 'Ariadne auf Naxos' from the wings. When a horrified Douglas Craig heard of this, he remarked 'I rather think that by now they imagine you are the Village Idiot from Glynde.'

The BBC recording of 'The Rake's Progress' at the end of the 1958 season was the midnight of my Cinderella experience and I was back (where I belonged) at the Ebbisham Hall.

o 0 o

For a couple of years in the early part of the 1960s the large storeroom above our shop at Ashtead Station became a mini film studio. Grandfather had built his shop and office upon land leased from the L.B. & S.C. Railway Company in November 1894. I still have the original agreement, which was periodically renewed till the 1970s. Matt Skipp of the Epsom Camera Club worked for Frank Woods of Waterloo Road at one of those Edwardian shops with the decorated fronts that still stand next to the space once occupied by the Foresters Hall. Matt was a very enthusiastic young man, quite determined about making an amateur film of one of Shakespeare's plays. He persuaded me to help him. We chose 'Julius Caesar' with me as Cassius and as the Director, and with absolutely no experience whatsoever of either. After two years of a lot of fun for a lot of people, our inability to dub the sound afterwards on to the unedited film in a way that we thought at all passable meant that the project had to be abandoned. What still exists might at least be an interesting relic for someone some day.

Whilst looking for the Ashtead document I have referred to, I also discovered the agreement dated 1905 between my grandfather and the L. & S.W. Railway Company to use, as pasture land for four pounds a year, that strip of land in Station Approach, Epsom – still called Waterloo Road then – opposite the station and on both sides of the alleyway to the High Street by the Clock Tower. I knew Grandfather kept pigs and sheep where Horsley Close and Hazon Way have now been built, but I did not previously realise he also did so on land to a depth of about eighty feet from the corner (marked Wesleyan Chapel on the plan) up to what is now Sainsbury's car park – and for only one pound quarterly.

o 0 o

Before turning to the more interesting buildings in South Street, Dorking Road and Woodcote, I might make mention of some of Epsom's hotels and public houses. The Tuns, which my father was able to remember but which had disappeared before my time, stood between The Marquis of Granby and The George. He was only able to tell me it advertised 'good beds'. Of the twenty seven pubs I once knew – thirteen of them in the town centre – nine no longer exist. The most notable losses from the centre have been The King's Head, The White Hart, The George and The Spread Eagle. The last mentioned most recently and most controversially.

Historically the most interesting was always The King's Head, where we now have the newest part of the Ashley Centre; for a short period earlier, the open King's Shades Walk. The Shades was once a separate little pub on the right. It was The King's Head where the Lords and Ladies of Charles the Second's time would stay. Pepys mentions it and for sure Nell Gwynne sometimes made use of it. If The King's Head was for the gentry, The Spread Eagle was what at one time, not so long ago, would have been termed 'family and commercial'. The former, on three levels connected by stairs and narrow passages, with many old oak beams, possessed a fine room some sixty feet in length, for balls and other special gatherings, which was added in the early nineteenth century. My own recollections of its interior are regrettably vague, even though it survived till 1957.

Father's patronage of Epsom's pubs would have produced little profit for publicans. His dislike of going into pubs, other than when away on holiday, was I suspect a legacy from his own father's Victorian puritanism. Grandfather witnessed and deplored much drunkeness during those forty years of his return to his native town. When on a certain Tuesday morning following a Bank Holiday one of his coalmen was still clearly unfit for work, he reproved him: 'Cuss it all, Fred, can't you have a holiday without getting drunk?' 'Not a good'un, Guv' was the reply; and Fred was, I am assured, only too typical. Of the interior of The Spread Eagle, unlike The King's Head, I have many pleasant memories. For a period I attended monthly meetings upstairs and remember thinking it must have been in the very same room that Benjamin Furniss went to his Masonic Lodge meetings over two hundred years earlier.

My meetings were on Thursdays, and each November it seemed to coincide with the Miss World Competition. My colleagues in 1968 were totally disbelieving when I told them that the glamorous Miss Costa Rica was my cousin. Maurice Furniss, a grandson of my grandfather's brother James, had in 1926 married a certain Margarita Segreda – in the Chapel of the Convent of the Sacred Hearts I was told – and before long a branch of our family was founded in Central America. Maurice's son, Jimmy, has eleven children and his daughter Elizabeth three and, when I last heard from that part of the world, a growing number of grandchildren. There are a lot more Furnisses in San José than Epsom.

Epsomians, if dismayed at the closure of The Spread Eagle, are at least relieved that the outward appearance of the old spa period hotel remains, as does the large eagle over the entrance. This is correctly coloured black. The original name was The Black Spread Eagle. The recently opened Spread Eagle Walk replaces the yard and stables.

I have been amused to see eighteenth and nineteenth century tradesmens' advertisements, referring to their prospective customers as 'the Nobility, the Gentry, the Clergy, members of the Medical Profession – and Others.'

Between The Albion and The Magpie was, till not many years ago, an alleyway known as The Folly – part of the old Epsom spa area. It was here Fred Ratcliffe, who has kindly given me interesting pieces of local information, was born in 1911. He tells me The Folly was regularly the scene of small fairs, even in his time. I have been reminded by him of the comparatively recent Tuttes Cafe and Sweet Shop by The Albion he used to frequent, and also memories of time spent in Wilfred Lovelock's gramophone shop opposite. Wilfred possessed a bass voice which could have been the envy of many a professional. The present Playhouse bar, which I regularly utilise for meetings (as well as a drink), I once knew as an antiques shop, but Fred as the abode of a Mr. Cook of earlier days. Fred is a member of an old Epsom family who lived mostly on the Common. His grandmother ran a laundry, near what was known as Ratcliffe's Pond, and her washing lines were a familiar sight to the Common dwellers.

He tells me a family neighbour, a certain Mr. Oakshott, who had a farm at the top of Wheelers Lane, was for a period the Lord of the Manor. It seems that on one occasion he failed to be allotted a seat in the Grand Stand, and threatened to exercise his manorial rights on the Downs to drive his sheep over the race course even on Derby Day if the Grand Stand seat was not forthcoming. Fred was a Post Office messenger boy from 1925 to 1928 and during that time had often witnessed a shepherd on the Downs working the sheep with his dog. He was fascinated. The training, showing and judging of dogs became his 45 year long hobby. He produced many a champion, won hundreds of awards, became a judge at national level, officiating on occasions at Crufts and on TV. His continued work for the Post Office as an engineer won him the Imperial Service Medal.

o 0 o

Between the town and the old wells on the Common many a large house and small cottage was built in the seventeenth and eighteenth centuries. By 1991 some have vanished, some remain virtually unaltered in so far as their exterior appearance is concerned, some have been partly rebuilt or enlarged. Starting from the town and going south, the small white weather-boarded cottage on the left – till recently Stebbings – is eighteenth century, and is now excellently repaired and repainted. Similar cottages are still to be found in both East Street and Hook Road near their junction, and also in Adelphi Road nearby.

Over the road, what is today an Italian restaurant has origins in the late 1600s. I recall it as Ivy Dene Tea Rooms. The new Ashley Avenue put an end to The Shrubbery of the seventeenth century. This was once a fine house with wrought iron railings leading up to an impressive door. It became very run down over the years behind a strip of long grass and weeds. Sean Kahn told me some years ago how keen he was to see restored the seventeenth century house that, standing well back from the road, had for so long, obscured by shops and a garage, been neglected and forgotten. This has now been excellently accomplished and as Winchester House, across Ashley Avenue from The Playhouse, is a fine example of a Stuart country house and also of good restoration. Before coming to The Queen's Head, there are two cottages, just below the level of the road, that date back to 1675. On the other side, Abele Cottages were of the same period but were much altered in late Victorian days. Woodcote Hall, on the corner of Woodcote Road, is again the late seventeenth century. A large building, converted into flats some time ago, this has had its ups and downs. Fortunately today it is in a much better condition – as is the space around it – than for a long time. The Convent of the Sacred Hearts School on the right, which has seen all our children in turn when little, has its base in Abele Grove, which in fact belongs to the early nineteenth century. The sisters now enjoy a large modern convent standing upon the green hill behind. On the right again is the Clock House, which has an impressive columned porch if one can see behind the wall. It was rebuilt, also early in the nineteenth century, by the Sir James Alexander to whom I have previously referred. As The Elms, the original was eighteenth century. Next door the Bell House with turret and clock is attractive. On the left of Dorking Road we have The White Horse Inn with origins back in the late 1600s. This was the New Inn of New Inn Lane. A little further up the hill is The Hylands and, standing back in an imposing position, Hylands House. Both are of bright red brick and of the mid-1700s. The latter was once the residence of Sir Thomas Bicknell, a High Court Judge. He was a prominent member of a number of Epsom clubs, including the Epsom Rifle Club, of which he was a founder in 1899. The painter John Constable lived there from 1809 to 1811. On the opposite side in White Horse Drive is the Rosebery Girls' School. Dorking Road still possesses a number of tall trees. From the period of the old wells, for more than a hundred years, limes and elms lined the whole of New Inn Lane.

Back in my early days in Worple Road I would be taken for walks to Woodcote. This was almost like going out into the country. Woodcote still retains something of a village appearance around a few fine late seventeenth to mid-eighteenth century houses, some rather pretty little cottages and two public houses. It was of course more like a separate village in the 1920s, except that there was no church and just one small general shop. There were no new houses on the right of the main road and there was only Major General Northey's Woodcote House, now hidden by trees and converted into flats, and the same little pond close by the road on the left.

Woodcote Road was a little used lane and Chalk Lane no more than a rough track. My walks would often include the secluded Madan's Walk, which still runs from Rosebery Park to the side of The Ladas – a pleasant tree-lined walkway and piece of old Epsom. The Rev. Martin Madan lived at Woodcote End House in the latter part of the eighteenth century and died there in 1790. It possesses a most attractive curved porch with columns. The Rev. Madan managed to achieve a certain amount of notoriety when it was claimed he had been, if not exactly advocating, at least in sympathy with polygamy. As a magistrate he also drew some unfavourable attention upon himself by trying to stop games being played in the High Street at race times. The actor, Sir Stanley Baker, lived here for a short time before his early death. The older part, now a separate home, is known as Queen Anne House. Somewhere hereabouts once lived for a while the famous singer, Clara Butt.

The public house on the corner of Woodcote Road and Chalk Lane was renamed The Ladas after Lord Rosebery's Derby success in 1894, when he was Prime Minister. Previously it was called The Fox and was the meeting place for the Masonic Lodge of Fortitude and Perseverence from 1770 to 1800. There was after that no masonic lodge in Epsom till the present Ebbisham Lodge was consecrated in 1829 meeting at The King's Head. More recently, the Prince of Wales Lodge dates only from 1926.

Up to the time that Sir Gilbert Heathcote won the Derby in 1838, The Amato in Chalk Lane was called the Hare and Hounds. The present building is of quite recent date, following a fire. There was a time when the name of a horse would be chalked on the well outside early each Derby Day and I saw this many times. It was, so I was told, originally supposed to be the inspired tip of a gipsy woman with fortune telling powers. I never heard what her success rate was.

Worple Road is much older than Woodcote Road and was the old way from Woodcote to the original Epsom. It was the continuation of Chalk Lane, the ancient sheep walk from the Downs.

The little shop opposite the end of Chalk Lane is a shop no longer but the attractive cottages remain, as do the well preserved line of seven eighteenth century cottages on the right entering Chalk Lane from Woodcote Green House.

What is now called Westgate House I remember as Woodcote Hotel. A mid-1920s advertisement I have boasts 'electric light throughout.' The large building, looking rather sad today, would date from the end of the seventeenth century.

From the Amato, by the much enlarged and popular Chalk Lane Hotel, whose origins go back for nearly three hundred years, we come to the really beautiful red brick Maidstone House, with its attractive courtyard and garden, on the right; and on the left the large seventeenth century Woodcote Grove, built by Josiah Diston in 1680. The entrance to this, and the rest of W. S. Atkins' considerable office buildings and grounds, is now in Ashley Road. The small rounded hill by Woodcote Grove was known as Mount Diston. I have already mentioned The Durdans in Chalk Lane, Woodcote House in Woodcote Road and Woodcote Park, much further up Wilmerhatch Lane.

o 0 o

One very wet morning early in 1963, standing on the corner by The Spread Eagle, I happened to meet John Gale. He was the Chairman of the Epsom Symphony Orchestral Society and the orchestra's conductor. I had, at that time, met him but briefly on a few occasions. In a few words (because it was raining) he told me he was very anxious to present opera at the Epsom Baths Hall with his orchestra, a locally recruited chorus and possibly a few professional singers in the principal roles. Would I like to consider how this might be done, with a view to acting as producer? – maybe Mozart's 'Magic Flute' to start with? I said 'yes' without hesitation (it was now raining harder than ever) and quickly walked back to the office with a head full of exciting ideas. Thus was born Grand Opera in Epsom and what, in a few more years, was to become Nonsuch Opera Society.

On the 30th of November 1963, one performance of 'The Magic Flute' before a well satisfied audience of some three hundred people took place. The chorus had been largely recruited from old friends in the Epsom Operatic Society and the principals supplied by Norman Lilley and Jean Buck of the London Opera Group, who at that time frequently presented opera in Epsom. For the 1964 production we became even more ambitious (some predicted over-ambitious) with two performances of Verdi's 'Aida', and a company of in all two hundred and seventeen. This included the Epsom Symphony Orchestra, a section of the British Legion Military Band, a stage chorus, balcony chorus, dancers, boys from a Borstal Institution as soldiers, and principals from the Glyndebourne Festival Opera Company, recruited by Susan Gray. The success of 'Aida' took everyone by surprise, including 'The Two Johns' as we were called. John Gale's mother, Edith (later Mrs. Tomlinson), was an inspiration throughout. She was the much respected 'mother' of the Epsom Symphony Orchestra till her death only a few years ago. For me, the old pioneer spirit of those early days has never quite been recaptured. Twenty-eight years later, twenty-eight Grand Operas have been presented, and I have been happy and grateful to have been entrusted with the direction of twenty three of them.

In 1968 the management of the E.S.O. decided to discontinue playing for the opera and concentrate again on their own programmes. This led to the formation of the Nonsuch Opera Society. Since 1988, under their present conductor, Darrell Davison, they have joined forces with Nonsuch Opera for one week each March. The E.S.O. has just in 1991 celebrated its ruby anniversary.

The Baths Hall was not everybody's idea of an Opera House, but it served us well for just on twenty years. I found the large open stage (as opposed to one enclosed by a proscenium) better for the spectacles our audiences wanted and came to expect. James Robertson, the conductor and principal of the London Opera Centre, was initially a great help. His students and former students provided many of the principals and in time it became very rewarding to see so many to whom we had given opportunities in our 'nursery' go on to achieve successes at the Royal Opera House, English National Opera, Glyndebourne, and abroad. I could furnish a most impressive list of some two dozen or so.

Quite by chance I was introduced by the Production Manager of the Old Vic, John Titcombe, who happened to live in Epsom's Lower Hill Road, to Leonard Tucker, the theatre's Chief Electrician. Len later became Lighting Manager of the National Theatre in its new South Bank home. He provided me not only with much technical advice but loads of equipment over the years, which had to be transported on Furniss' coal lorries. He also provided me with a fascinating number of visits back stage at both of the National's sites, including the unusual view of Olivier's 'Othello' from the lighting control position.

Over the years Nonsuch Opera has made practically all its own costumes and scenery and, thanks to a number of most devoted and hard working people, still does so. The unusual costume store in our large attic at home grows larger and better; much thanks being due to the energy and efficiency of the Wardrobe Mistress, Joy Foreman.

'A funny thing happened on my way to the theatre,' is the comedian's traditional line. Needless to say, plenty of funny things happened over the years inside our theatre. In Gounod's 'Faust' it is necessary to have an organ for the church scene. At the dress rehearsal in 1965, before the days of mini-sized electronic instruments, we had an enormous wooden contraption, which must have weighed several hundredweight, somehow heaved up the Baths Hall front steps and wheeled into position next to the conductor. It was to be played by its owner, who lovingly called the thing 'Johosophat'. At the dress rehearsal our organist disappeared for a couple of hours before returning in time for his big scene. In the meantime he had presumably spent his time at The Queen's Arms, which at that time was just opposite. He tottered down the main aisle, uneasily mounted the organ stool, had some difficulty in sorting out his music and a great deal more in playing it. When the conductor, John Gale, had failed, the task of bringing him in in the right place was taken on jointly by 'Mephistopholes' and 'Margarita'. This comic trio was watched with apprehension and amusement by the orchestra, the chorus and the rest of us. Eventually he began. After a few notes he fell right off the stool on to the organ pedals, producing sounds that Gounod could never have written nor imagined. Felton Rapley was hurriedly engaged for the following evening and, as one would expect from so distinguished an organist, played the church scene to perfection. However, for the change of scene music that followed, Felton gave one of his great virtuoso performances, creating fantastic effects but all at about double speed, completely upsetting the Stage Manager's technical arrangements. Late on the Saturday night, as 'Johosophat' was finally wheeled away, John Gale, to round off the whole affair of the erring organist, announced – rather oddly I thought – 'Well, he was a Doctor of Music'.

Nigel Brooks, creator of the Nigel Brooks Singers, who still lives in Epsom, was one of the Society's Musical Directors. He was followed by Nina Walker, at the time a repetiteur at the Royal Opera House and subsequently Chorus Master of the Royal Choral Society and the Huddersfield Choral Society. Fraser Goulding, after two seasons, had to leave to take up his appointment as Musical Director of the D'Oyly Carte Company and is now appearing frequently at the Royal Festival Hall and the Barbican Hall. At the time Nonsuch Opera finally had to leave the Baths Hall, the Musical Director was a young Andrew Greenwood of Covent Garden Opera, subsequently with the Welsh National Opera. The Society provided, therefore, a useful platform for professional conductors as well as for up-and-coming professional singers.

o 0 o

I had occasion in 1964 to attend a dinner at the R.A.C., and there on the top table, side by side, were two gentlemen with the Epsom connection but of opposite political colour. Neither made a speech, that duty falling upon the wife of one of them, Mrs. Laura Woodcock, who was our Mayor at the time.

Peter Rawlinson was created a Baron and became Lord Rawlinson of Ewell in 1978. He had been called to the bar in 1946, a Q.C. since 1959, knighted in 1962 and a Privy Councillor in 1964. He was our Member of Parliament from 1955 to 1978, during which time he was the Solicitor General from 1962 to 1964 and Attorney General from 1970 to 1974. I had heard him speak but once, with the impressive fluency and charm one would have expected, and if I do not now recall what he said I am sure that is my loss. George Woodcock was Assistant Secretary to the T.U.C. from 1947–1960, a CBE in 1953, Privy Councillor in 1967 and the General Secretary of the T.U.C. from 1960–1969. He lived in Lower Hill Road and died in 1979. As I remember him, George Woodcock had big bushy eyebrows and a rather troubled mien that could well have been caused by the considerable responsibilities of his job. The mien, not the eyebrows.

o 0 o

Before concluding the 1960s, I must mention an Epsom 'spectacular' that was produced by accident. Just after lunchtime one day in the spring of 1969, as I walked down to the back door of our shop, I noticed what I thought was a puff of smoke emerging from the side of the large barn in the yard. It was in this old building, erected some time in the era of G. & J. Furniss about the middle of the last century and that had in its time stored carts and building materials, that we kept our hay and straw. There were also thousands of firelighters and a large tank of paraffin. Upon investigation it was indeed smoke that was coming from the straw. A 999 call brought two fire engines with commendable promptness, by which time there had been no stopping the fire with our puny extinguishers. It was a terrific blaze. As thousands of gallons of water were hosed upon it by a number of firemen, some of whom seemed quite excited to have a really good fire at last, people began to gather. Flames shot up many feet into the air, things hissed and popped; timber and corrugated iron crashed down. I did not blame the crowd for enjoying it, but did, at such an emotional moment, resent the pressing opportunism of the demolition contractors and insurance assessors. I had collected cards from the touts long before the firemen had finished their work. Months later, of course, there was the 'small print' to contend with, but a surprise cheque about a year later concluded the matter reasonably. The quotations for the demolition costs, by the way, varied by over six hundred per cent. If you want to have a really good fire, try a mixture of hay, straw, firelighters and paraffin.

# Chapter Seven

Epsomians, generally speaking, are not greatly interested in horse racing; the Downs are just taken for granted. John Toland, who lived in Woodcote in the early part of the eighteenth century, wrote: 'The Downs being covered with grass finer than Persian carpets, and perfumed with wild thyme and juniper . . . for sheep walks, riding, hunting, racing and shooting, with games of most sorts for exercising of the body and recreation of the mind . . . they are nowhere else to be paralleled.' For Epsom people today they mean fresh air, wonderful views and an open space to walk with the children or the dogs.

As well as the Downs itself, there are pleasant walks up from the town via Chalk Lane or the footpath between Downs and Burgh Heath Roads to the site of the old Rifle Butts (not used since the days of the 1914–18 war); also from the valley on the south side to Tadworth through woods or up the old and muddy sheep walk to Headley Park. Weekends attract hundreds of cars. Riding is increasingly popular.

Racing to most people means The Derby – and that means the extraordinary annual carnival and unique occasion. Where else on earth could you find at one time a quarter of a million people so diverse as the Queen and members of the Royal Family, gypsies, fortune tellers and tipsters from the most down at heel to the most elaborate, leading and lesser politicians, owners, trainers, jockeys, lads and officials, film stars, stage stars, television personalities and those many others dressed up determined to be noticed, police and pickpockets, fairground folk with their incredible caravans, sophisticated machines and tatty stalls, the aristocratic in their top hats and the not-so-aristocratic in their Moss Bros. suits, vulgar jolly nobodies, nondescript Londoners on a day out, locals on their once-a-year pilgrimage, sellers and consumers of bottled beer and stout, bookies and tic-tac men, people in buses, coaches, cars, lorries, ambulances and helicopters, mothers with babies in their prams and Rolls Royces with champagne in their boots – all jammed and jostling, inextricably mixed? That's Derby Day.

I am pleased to say the people of Epsom are assured their freedom to enjoy the Downs now and in the future. Long ago Walter Langlands, Henry Mayson Dorling and Earle Dorling purchased, for the Epsom Grand Stand Association, the freehold of the Downs from the Lord of the Manor for some £57,000, and subsequently sold the training grounds on the Walton Manor Estate to Stanley Wootton, the trainer and magistrate. Stanley Wootton was the brother of Frank Wootton, a successful jockey. Their father originally came from Australia.

The 1936 Epsom and Walton Downs Regulation Act states, 'Epsom Downs and a portion of Walton Downs are the property of the Epsom Grand Stand Association Ltd., and a further portion of Walton Downs is the property of Stanley Wootton'; also 'The Epsom and Ewell Urban District Council claim that members of the public have a right of access for air and exercise over the whole of the said Downs'; and also 'The Downs from the enactment of the Act shall be regulated, preserved and controlled by a body corporate with perpetual succession styled the Epsom and Walton Downs Conservators.' Members of our Borough Council are included in the above and in 1984 the Act further extended the freedom of all people to use our wonderful Downs.

John Toland, when living in Woodcote, wrote: '. . . thus when you are on top of the downs 'tis one of the loveliest prospects imaginable, to view in the vale below such an agreeable mixture of trees and buildings, that a stranger is at a loss to know whether it be a town in a wood or a wood in a town.' One of the most agreeable thoughts today, some two hundred and seventy years later, is that to some extent the same may still be said. Some of the larger of Epsom's buildings show up from the Downs, but on the whole it is still mainly trees of which we are conscious in the general landscape.

Races in some form or another seem to have taken place since the time of our first Stuart monarch, whether they were between the servants of the great houses on foot or between the owners themselves on horseback. The popularity of the sport of horse racing on the Downs grew considerably in parallel with that of the taking of Epsom's waters.

On the twenty-fifth of July 1663 Samuel Pepys wrote, 'Having intended this day to go to Banstead Downs to see a famous race, I sent Will to get himself ready to go with me; but I hear it is put off because the Lords do sit in Parliament today.' All west of Woodmansterne was once known as Banstead Downs.

The story told by Pepys, when writing of the fourteenth of July 1667, of the shepherd and his boy is quite charming. The shepherd wore 'woolen knit stockings of two colours mixed.' His shoes were 'shod with iron both at the toe and the heels.' He had, we learn, an efficient sheep dog, about three hundred and fifty sheep, and was paid four shillings a week throughout the year for his work. I particularly like the pretty picture painted of the shepherd's little boy reading the bible to his father and then to Pepys himself, 'with that forced tone that children do usually read.'

The next century saw far more racing. The famous horse, Eclipse (foaled in the year of the Great Eclipse, 1764), was acquired by a certain Irishman, 'Colonel' O'Kelly, who had arrived in Epsom in the 1770s, and trained for racing. Kelly's stables and paddocks, covering some ten acres, were by the Warren on the Walton side of the Downs. His elegant house of 1785 was on Clay Hill (now called West Hill) where Kingswood House School now stands. O'Kelly was a rough diamond, but with the ability – probably resented – to push himself into the company of the rich and powerful and obviously the ability to train a horse. He seems to have purchased the rank of 'Colonel' to give himself some importance.

Eclipse, of whom it was said four miles could be covered in eight minutes, was never beaten. He was tried out at Epsom for the first time in 1769. Many a Derby winner since has been a descendant of that great animal.

The second Eclipse public house at the foot of West Hill has only in the last few years closed down. The original was destroyed by fire over a hundred years ago.

The site of the Warren can be found among the trees not far from the top of Beaconsfield Road by the recreation ground. Originally it was connected with the sport of hare coursing and subsequently made into a hunting lodge for Charles the Second. Much later again, in the nineteenth century, it was utilised in connection with horse racing. Nothing now remains of the house.

The story of the famous dinner party at The Oaks, near Woodmansterne, on the evening of the 14th of May 1779 has been told many a time; and of how the Derby might have been called the Bunbury. In point of fact it might well have been called the Burgoyne, or the Grafton, or the Sheridan, or perhaps the Eclipse (not the O'Kelly by any means), but according to the tale, which the present Lord Derby seems to accept, the coin when tossed came down in favour of the 12th Earl. And what a picture it conjures up – of rich young sportsmen, soldiers and gamblers, with wine, women and song, all noisily celebrating together in alcoholic revelry. This was the dinner after the running of the first Oaks. The first Derby was run the following year and won by a horse called Diomed, owned by Sir Charles Bunbury.

Up to about this time horses had raced over quite long distances of several miles. For instance, a race might be from Woodmansterne to somewhere near today's finishing post. The present public house, The Rubbing House, takes its name from the old building where the horses were rubbed down. I knew this as the Downs Hotel in the days of Mrs. Clarke. It was men like Edward Stanley (who became Lord Derby) and Bunbury who changed the style of racing by training their horses to run much faster but over shorter distances. The original Derby course was actually of one straight mile. A few years later it was changed to one and a half miles (as at present) over a 'U' shaped course. The exact 'high level' course of today was first used for the Derby of 1872. Although the Derby is a so-called 'flat' race, there is nothing very flat about this unique Epsom course, which possesses in all rises of over one hundred and fifty feet, including a gradient of 1 in 18 over the initial 500 yards.

The popularity of the annual event grew, and within a few years some five thousand spactators were attending. By the time Queen Victoria paid her one and only visit in 1840 the number was estimated at one hundred and fifty thousand. Charles Dickens wrote a rather excitable piece on the subject in 1851, referring to the 'huge white object' (the Grand Stand), to the 'Great Man' (the Clerk of the Course), to 'Dorling's correct list' (the race card) and, most mouth wateringly, to 'champagne and Fortnum and Mason's hampers.' He did as well manage to include 'the Glorious Race'.

I always liked the look of the old white Grand Stand when I was a boy. There was something exciting as well as beautiful and elegant about it (Dickens' 'large white object'). This was the 1828 stand as enlarged in 1886. It was built for £14,000 for the new Epsom Grand Stand Association and held some seven and a half thousand people, of whom one-third were obliged to remain in the open on the roof. There are plenty of good photographs of it in books – and many more in Epsomians' albums or attics I expect. Before 1828 there would have been only the original Princes Stand and the wooden Rubbing House. Today's Princes Stand was built in 1879, following a fire which destroyed the old. This remains, even though it accommodates very few spectators, doubtless for sentimental reasons.

The Downs had its first railway station in 1865. This was, and is, a terminus on the line from Sutton and Banstead and it had as many as nine platforms. Epsom Downs Station has, only in the last few years, been rebuilt further back down the line, making space for a number of new houses bordering the Downs. Tattenham Corner Station, on the line from Caterham and Tadworth, dates only from 1901.

1914 saw the erection of the large building to the rear of the Grandstand, which was immediately used as a war hospital. It was here I performed in a concert which, bad though it must have been, seemed to amuse a rowdy band of young soldiers stationed there very early in the next world war.

The present large Grand Stand, some seventy feet high and well over a hundred yards long, was, I remember, much criticised at the time of its building in 1926/27 as being anything but beautiful and elegant. Together with the Club Stand and the East Stand twenty thousand people could be accomodated. Today as a result of considerable re-development and re-decoration, a new enlarged multi-purpose Club Stand has been built, together with a much improved roadway layout. The attractive modern stand was opened by The Queen on Derby Day 1992, and has met with wide approval and praise.

My own attendances at Epsom Races pre-war were confined to the latter 1930s. People used to say it always rained at the Spring Meeting – just as it was said Wimbledon fortnight was always hot and sunny. Neither were true. I saw the Great 'Met' – the only race partly run off the regular course to achieve the two and a quarter miles distance, and initiated by Samuel Beeton (Grandfather of the Sam who married Isabella) in 1846 – at least twice on warm sunny April days and, on one occasion, the Derby on a bitterly cold one in overcoat and scarf. The Derby was once actually run in snow.

Since the war, I estimate I have been present at twenty-seven Derbys, especially enjoying the carnival spirit, the crowds, the colour and the tension just before the big race itself. I could never have experienced such excitement as my parents did when I was away at school in 1932. That year Tom Walls won with his April the Fifth. I am told the noisy celebrations at North Looe, almost opposite us in the Reigate Road, continued well into the night. For Tom Walls acting was his job – racing was his love.

I had the unusual win of a few pounds – something that has not resulted since from my modest once-a-year flutter of a few 'bob' – on the very first occasion post war. We stuck one of Peter's nappy pins into the list in the morning paper and managed to prick Airborne – at 66 to 1.

I used to go home to lunch each day over the chalkpit hill and down the Reigate Road from the Drift Bridge. On one Derby Day – it must have been between 1947 and 1951 – when I got to within about five hundred yards of home, I was approached at great speed by a lone motorcycle policeman, who urgently waved me to a stop. Before he reached me I had already noticed a huge tree had fallen right across the road and thought how efficient (even kind) it was of him to warn me. Within a few seconds of coming to a standstill, only a few feet in front of me, and driving out of Mizens Market Gardens, came a large black Rolls Royce, containing unmistakably His Majesty King George the Sixth with the Queen and the two Princesses. The King acknowledged my surprising presence with a sort of nod and the Queen with the smile she still kindly bestows upon we lowly folk some forty years on. I regret to report our present Sovereign and her sister were what could only be described as stoney-faced. I proceeded – via Mizens – to my shepherd's pie and they to their salmon and champagne – or was it Malvern Water?

Older people tend to say, 'Things ain't what they used to be,' usually inferring that 'things' are now a lot worse. No doubt this is largely illusionary: memory is rather kind. I would certainly not be one to insist that all the old atmosphere and glamour has gone for ever. There is still much of the same remaining to be enjoyed from the unique occasion. The fair in the dip in the centre of the course has disappeared. It was here, even in my early days, that many a good carthorse or pony was sold. The 'gypsies' are less genuine and more motorised, show booths have been largely replaced by commercial stalls and there are now less of those colourful tipsters and amusing entertainers. And, of course, there is no be-feathered Prince Monolulu.

In recent years I have, more often than not, taken up my position on the first Wednesday in June just opposite the Princes Stand where, without seeing much of the race itself, one can view at close range the Queen and members of the Royal Family on their way to and from the paddock, see the parade of horses before the event and finally the leading-in of the winner. About three years ago a 'bunny girl' from the VIP area in front of me jumped over the rails and ran out between the rows of police to present a flower to the Queen, who received it with surprise and the famous smile. The 'bunny girl' did a little curtsey and ran back laughing. Not one of the police, nor the plain clothes men, nor anyone else took the slightest notice. Over the years I have seen Lester Piggott win six times, Willie Carson win Derby 200 in 1979 and Shergar win by the greatest ever margin, but, like so many of my friends in the town, am not a racing man. I know little about it professionally.

South Hatch, near the top of Burgh Heath Road, was occupied by the Nightingall family from 1860, when it was acquired by the trainer, Arthur Nightingall. His son William, who was born at South Hatch, was a good steeplechase jockey before following his father as a trainer. William's son was Walter, who will be well and kindly remembered by many Epsomians today. His riding days were short-lived but he was most successful as a trainer. He trained for Dorothy Paget, winning the 1943 Derby (at Newmarket), and after 1949 for none other than Winston Churchill. I had occasion to call on Walter Nightingall once on business and was most courteously invited in for tea. This was taken in a most elegant drawing room, in company with members of his family and some professional friends. I remember how ill-at-ease I felt. I had little in common with the rest, whose conversation centred almost entirely upon what had happened at Sandown Park, or this that and the other horse. I contributed little; however, the tea and cakes were nice and I enjoyed it more in retrospect. Walter died in 1968 and South Hatch is now run as a restaurant and club.

o 0 o

Right at the top of Longdown Lane South and on the fringe of the Downs is the Epsom Golf Club House, built in 1892.

It was in the very early days of the nineteenth century that golf was believed to have been played in the area of the Grand Stand and the Rifle Butts. A little pioneering by some of the masters of Epsom College led to a meeting at Bromley Hurst in 1889 and to the formation of the Epsom Golf Club, well-known today. It is, in fact, one of the oldest in the country.

Early Vice-Presidents were Lord Rosebery and the Rev. E. W. Northey – those two names recurring so frequently in our town's history.

At the time of the club's centenary, a booklet, 'A Reflection on the First 100 Years', was produced and from that I was interested to learn that ladies were admitted as associate members in 1909, but that even in the 1930s and 40s were restricted to the use of a small wooden hut quite apart from the Club House. It appears they were not emancipated till 1960. It was in that year when club membership had reached a very low level that the new Captain, Epsom-born Michael Everett, became a leading figure in staging a revival. As an estate agent he had just sold the Granada Cinema in Church Street and was presented, to help the golf club, with all the cinema restaurant furniture. The ladies section were then given permission to use the Club House with its refurbished lounge and bar.

o 0 o

The mile-and-a-half race course starts a little way down the hill into the valley at the western end of the Downs, thus giving an uphill ride for the first half mile. This, together with the unusually steep sharp curve of Tattenham Corner, followed by an abrupt rise over the final furlong, is what makes our Derby course such an exacting test. The valley to the west towards the Headley Road was called Langley Bottom when I was younger. The residents, who perhaps considered the anatomical connotation of 'bottom' unbecoming as an address, now live in Langley Vale.

It was here that in pre-war years a certain Phyllis Dixey lived. Miss Dixey was a stage artiste, quite celebrated in the specialised art of taking off her clothes and appearing in the nude. It was all very artistically done of course, in suitably dim lighting and, in accordance with the Lord Chamberlain's regulations, without the moving of a muscle. I remember in this connection the saying, 'If you move it's rude.'

A theatrical resident of today, most happily remembered for the particular comic clothes he kept on and for moving about rather a lot, is Norman Wisdom, who has a flat in Church Street. Another comedian with the Epsom connection is Freddie Sales, who has spent many years of late on the other side of the Atlantic but was formerly most successful over here. He still has a house in Woodcote and, I am pleased to say, keeps in touch with me and my family. I am told the old music hall and wireless comedian Harry Tate used to live in Epsom, and I have recently met someone who remembers his car with the registration number T.8.

o 0 o

In November 1980 I received a letter commencing, 'You have never heard of me, whereas I have collected quite a lot of information about the Furniss family in Epsom.' The writer, Fred Baylis of Reading, turned out to be a quite unknown second cousin, being the grandson of my Furniss grandfather's sister. Fred, after concluding his studies of the Baylis family, had apparently started on the Furniss family tree and was obviously very good at the job. We communicated all through 1981, although meeting only on one occasion. He was able to correct a few of my misconceptions on the first part of the eighteenth century, but more importantly could supply much earlier information than I had been able to discover. Whereas my family tree began with the arrival in Epsom from Ewell of John Furniss in 1716, he was able to go back as far as 1585. Unfortunately, Fred died not long after I had discovered him and, in fact, 1585 still remains our family history starting point. That ancestor, who certainly lived in Ewell even before the days of the Spanish Armada, was called Ralph. Actually the spelling used at the time of the baptism of his first child, Mary, in 1610 was Rayffe ffurnisse. He had a further two daughters and three sons. One of the sons died in infancy, and of another there is no information after his birth. It must have been Richard, born in 1621 and married to Mary King of Banstead, who was the father of the John Furniss born in 1660, himself the father of the second John of 1684, after whom I was named. From Ralph (Rayffe) to my grandchildren we can, therefore, now record, over a period of four hundred and seven years, as many as twelve generations of the family in Epsom and Ewell.

o 0 o

In the 1970s oil prices were pushed up to the extent that our firm's heating oil business, which had been slowly increasing for ten years, now rapidly decreased. Large garden centres began to spring up everywhere. Our small garden shop at 100 High Street became but a place to pick up the little thing that had been forgotten, or the unusual item that was not available at the garden centre. We tried a little diversification, like the five-gallon paraffin drum delivery service from the Epsom yard and the agency for Epsom Coaches at the Banstead office.

Epsom Coaches had been expanding for some years and their dark red coaches a familiar sight on our roads. It was in 1920 that H. R. Richmond first had a char-a-banc operating in our town. The son of a Norfolk farmer, he became interested in engineering and in the first world war, having already transferred his attention from farm equipment to road vehicles, now worked on aircraft. Following an association with Tommy Sopwith at Kingston after the 1914–18 war, he came to Epsom and soon had six char-a-bancs and six horse boxes operating from a yard at the rear of the old Boots at the narrow end of the High Street. In those days horses were still, in the main, transported by rail and I well remember the horse dock by the side of the road at Epsom Station. In time Wootton, Duller, Ingham and all the various Smythes began to use Richmond's horse boxes. Richmonds then moved to a yard in South Street where Waitrose's service area is now. Roy Richmond has recently reminded me of the Epsom County School for Boys in Church Street, where he was a pupil and which I had quite forgotten. He went into his father's business in 1947 and has been in control of the growing Epsom Coaches – and later of Epsom Travel – since the 1960s. Their current depot in Longmead opened in 1970 and Epsom Buses came into operation in 1986. Roy was recently awarded the OBE.

o 0 o

My brother Bob and I finally retired on the first of February 1983, and sadly that six sided trade mark, with FURNISS in white block letters on a red background that had been designed by our grandfather in the 1870s and been so familiar on Epsom buildings and on Epsom vehicles for over a hundred years, now disappeared from the scene.

Being a coal merchant had been on the whole a rather unglamorous sort of occupation, providing little in the way of comic relief. I had on occasions to go out to investigate complaints and once made the mistake of doing so wearing my best dark blue suit and carrying a small black bag. I was met at the door by a lady who anxiously ushered me straight upstairs; an unusual location for the boiler I thought. 'In there,' she said, indicating what proved to be a bedroom. 'In there' was another lady in bed. It was discovered I was not the expected doctor before I had been invited to make a diagnosis, and in some confusion I left without finding out what was wrong with the boiler either.

Apart from Pullingers Ltd. (Dorlings), Lester Bowden Ltd., Michael Everett and Co., and Anderson's, I think all the private businesses I used to know in years gone by have now disappeared from the centre of the town. Over a period of twenty years or so others have been squeezed out either into the side streets or simply into the memories of older Epsomians or just a few lines of local history.

During the 1970's and early 1980's, the minds of those of us working, or living, in the centre of the town were very much occupied with the possibility or impossibility, and the desirability or undesirability of creating a large modern shopping centre on the south side of the western end of the High Street. Controversial argument ensued in the press, offices, bars, clubs and, no doubt, golf courses – would it make Epsom? – would it ruin Epsom? The association of the Borough Council, Bredero and the Friends Provident settled the matter, and behind the line of existing shops slowly the monster grew, the 1930s houses in the original cul-de-sac of Ashley Avenue having been demolished. The new Ashley Avenue was built, Petrofina (UK) Ltd., who some years before had had their regional office in Church Street, now commanded most of the frontage, with the multi-storey car park and the new theatre occupying the South Street corner.

In company with other interested people, I had some time earlier been asked to discuss and give views on a possible theatre in the town to replace the Ebbisham Hall. Subsequently, the council members considered various names such as the 'Spa', the 'Ebbisham', the 'Downs' and so forth. If not over imaginative, the choice of The Playhouse was not controversial. As always seems to be the case, it did not in the end appear that the requirements of producers or actors were really seriously entertained. The seating capacity, general appearance, dressing rooms, comfort and some technical aspects were all, unfortunately, criticised at the time. Although disapproval of some facets remain, the passage of time has brought acceptance of others and many improvements have certainly been made. It is interesting to note that the capacity of the 1929 Ebbisham Hall was over six hundred (reduced to just under six hundred subsequently by fire regulations). Fifty five years later, for a much grown town, The Playhouse was given a seating capacity in the region of four hundred. The theatre was opened in October 1984 (with the rest of the Ashley Centre). It was a great compliment to our Borough Council and to our popular Town Clerk, Douglas Grimes, now retired, that it should have been opened by none other than The Queen.

Purely in the matter of seating capacity, therefore, The Playhouse did not replace the Ebbisham Hall, as was always promised. The old building was a multi-purpose hall and I have already enumerated some of its many uses. The new building, even with the facility of the movability of many of the seats to form a small flat-floored central space, was always, in the main, going to be only a fairly conventional theatre. The old Myers Hall disappeared with the Ebbisham Hall. A new Myers Hall was incorporated into the new building, but this again did not replace the former facilities, where there were once two halls, a committee room and a toilet. What was really needed – and many feel still is – was the addition of a general purpose public hall – somewhere for concerts, fairs, parties, exhibitions, rehearsals, meetings and so on.

Within a few years W. S. Atkins, already utilising a considerable area between Ashley Road and Chalk Lane but required to expand even further, built a huge new block on the Rosebery Park side of the new Ashley Avenue. This was opened by Sir William Atkins in 1989. Some people are enthusiastic about the modern design and applaud the large glass central section in particular; others hate the whole thing. Those feeling disapproval here may perhaps derive some aesthetic pleasure from the later building adjacent – the new headquarters of Woodstock Land – offering a sympathetic frontage on to Rosebery Park. Nearby is the mid-Victorian Swail House, on the corner of Ashley and Heathcote Roads; for some years now much used and much appreciated as the centrepiece of accomodation and services for the blind, and having the distinction of being the first of such anywhere to be purpose-built.

Of the Ashley Centre, once it was completed there seemed to be almost universal approval; perhaps not of the lack of variety of the shops included but most certainly of the good design, brightness, cleanliness and security. The lifts, though attractive, are hardly big enough to accommodate the large number of shopping trolleys people try to jam into them. The car park, with the five lifts connecting it to the shops, is always popular – sometimes packed.

At the time of the coming into being of The Epsom Playhouse, the Council appointed Graham Stansfield as Borough Arts and Entertainments Officer. He, presumably with the best of intentions, seemed determined to provide programmes with what could only be termed a 'highbrow' emphasis. These the local people found to be more 'arty' than entertaining. Regrettably he also had the tendency to look down on amateurs who, in fact, had been providing most of the entertainment at the Ebbisham Hall for years. Professionals were engaged, irrespective of any possible popular appeal, whilst amateurs were reluctantly 'fitted in' if space permitted. String quartets, solo recitals and the like played largely to empty seats. The public did not want to be 'educated' and much money was lost. The Playhouse, therefore, got off to a rather bad start. It took a long time – a few years in fact – to reverse the trend and to establish something like the variety and balance we now enjoy.

o 0 o

By 1984 I had already given a number of talks on the history of the town, which I was pleased to find were being well received. I now wondered if I could combine this with my experience on the stage and dare to write and produce a revue. Being given much encouragement and help from many good friends – actors, singers, dancers, musicians and technicians – the result was 'Epsom Revued', advertised as 'a light hearted history of Epsom with a look at some of its famous, infamous and eccentric characters over the centuries'. John Gale wrote original and provided much recorded music. Greta Cresswell and Margaret Hunter of the Heath Players were most valuable associate directors. With a large cast of over fifty, we played to over a thousand people in February 1985. Douglas Grimes, the Town Clerk and Chief Executive, was throughout most supportive and asked me to produce a booklet of the script. This I did and it was printed by the Council.

I reproduce here the four verses of the topical song I performed in the revue, together with the notes that preceded them in the booklet:

Here are a few notes on the verses that follow. 1. 'Merry Widows' refers to the famous Operetta first produced in England in 1907. 2. The Mayor was Councillor Norma Fryer, who attended the final performance. There had been some controversy regarding the purchase of a new Rolls Royce for the Mayors of Epsom and Ewell. The Epsom Protection Society was in the middle of a well publicised campaign to plant trees in the Borough. The Town Clerk was Mr Douglas Grimes. 3. The Ebbisham Hall, which had served the town so well since 1929, had just been pulled down. Bredero was the name of the developers of the site which included the Ebbisham Hall, the Ashley Centre and the Epsom Playhouse. The Playhouse had been criticised for too many, so called, 'high-brow' programmes. The Saturday morning show for children was Mr Punch's Sausage and Custard Club. The Borough Arts and Entertainments Officer was Mr Graham Stansfield. There had been controversy, much written-up in the local papers, concerning the purchase of a £14,000 piano for the new theatre. 4. The building of the M25 had been temporarily halted. Traffic was an increasing problem. The Queen opened the Ashley Centre on 24 October 1984 – and it poured with rain all day.

Verse 1.

In the elegant haze
Of Edwardian days
With chorus girls stately and charming
Merry Widows would sing
In some sweet pretty thing
With an infantile plot – quite alarming.
About nineteen-o-five
To keep such shows alive
The topical song was invented
And they thought it all right
With new verses each night
Till the author was driven demented.

Peace, Peace,
They entitled it Peace
That most famous topical song
And the words every time
Of the very last line
Were 'the beautiful valley of Bong'.

Verse 2.

When you're writing the song
Mustn't put a foot wrong
Or be guilty of plugs too commercial
You're a fool if you dare
To poke fun at the Mayor
Or at Councillors (too controversial)
And don't act like those souls
Who begrudge her the Rolls
Just behave with the greatest propriety
Hold your tongue if you please
Don't go on about Trees
Like the Epsom Protection Society.

Peace, Peace,
Don't give them a piece
Of your mind when you're writing the song
Though I've tried many times
To think what rhymes with Grimes
But it isn't The Valley of Bong.

Verse 3.

Once the Ebbisham Hall
Was the mecca of all
With dramatic or musical inkling
And we trod on those boards
Till the Bredero hordes
Just demolished the lot in a twinkling
Now on quartets of strings
And such similar things
We put a bold face – keen as mustard –
Though an oboe recital
May seem rather vital
We prefer Punch's Sausage and Custard.

Peace, Peace,
Let this ribaldry cease
And we hope that our Stansfield's not wrong
Though pianos aren't found
At fourteen thousand pound
In the beautiful valley of Bong.

Verse 4.

Though the M25
Is more dead than alive
The traffic in South Street's increasing
Upper High Streets all cusses
With lorries and buses
Advice to the Councils unceasing
When the Queen promised rashly
To open our Ashley
The Town Clerk omitted to tell her,
Who usually most posh is,
To wear her galoshes
And come with her biggest umbrella.

Peace, Peace, the thanks never cease
Of all we subservient throng
For bringing her here
And for raising a cheer
They could hear in the Valley of Bong.

Two years later the Borough celebrated its first fifty years. I wrote and produced a further revue entitled – rather obviously – 'Golden Jubilee'. This was really a musical comedy version of a potted history of Epsom and Ewell. Margaret Hunter, Susan Gray and Derek Brown were, with me, the principals; Richard Fentiman's group 'Spectrum' sang; Lorna McGrath's girls danced and Rodney Lucas was again in charge of a great deal of recorded music. This took place at The Playhouse in February. It was in September 1987 that the Borough's official events were held, some in a large marquee at the Hook Road Arena in, disappointingly, rather cold and damp weather.

From this time onwards I found myself being more frequently invited to give talks on the history of Epsom and its inhabitants. The presentation was then improved by my having made nearly a hundred slides. By visiting many societies and clubs I have certainly increased my own knowledge and, I hope, engendered greater interest in others. More recently I have added musical recordings to extend these presentations to include musical comedy or Gilbert and Sullivan or opera.

Since the decision to provide all the year round swimming at the Baths, the closure of the hall for all those winter activities that used to take place there has meant that theatrical productions have, almost entirely, been transferred to The Playhouse. This has certainly created a much more 'professional' feel to the proceedings, especially with the presence of the ever efficient (and ever friendly) Technical Manager, Stan Masters. Perhaps, however, it's all a little less fun; even though I must say I have met with nothing but helpfulness and smiles from the people who work there. After eight years the place has become such a popular 'Mecca' for local companies that it is now difficult to obtain a booking.

I myself have undertaken only three of Nonsuch Opera's productions since 1983. My one and only return to the realm of Gilbert and Sullivan, after some twenty years, was 'The Yeomen of the Guard', with Fraser Goulding (by then the former Musical Director of D'Oyly Carte) as Conductor. It was a great pleasure to welcome Fraser back to Epsom and to have in the cast three of his old D'Oyly Carte principals. One little piece of information that interested me was recently provided by Martin Northey. It appears that Major General Sir Edward Northey so loved Gilbert and Sullivan that he presented his general's plumed hat to the D'Oyly Carte Company, who proceeded to use it for some years in 'The Pirates of Penzance' – strange that just some weeks before I had already written that his grandfather was 'the very model of a modern Major General'.

In 1988 the Epsom Symphony Orchestra renewed its association with Nonsuch Opera after a gap of exactly twenty years. The orchestra, under its popular conductor Darrell Davison, has made great strides in recent years and now enjoys a high reputation, with more numerous concerts, a wider range of music and good audiences at the Epsom Playhouse and other venues. Darrell, who read music at Cambridge and won the Barbirolli conducting competition subsequently, is now the Musical Director of several organisations. The E.S.O's leader, Eric Hastings, is to be found in orchestra pits for various companies, and his broad smile and friendly wave must be familiar to many concert goers.

It was a great pleasure for me to have in 'Aida' in 1989 ten dancers from the Laine Theatre Arts organisation. Many years ago I met Jean Frecker when she was still a dance student. Subsequently I was to be associated with her on a few occasions. The Jean Frecker School of Dancing, so well-known over many years in Epsom, was a few years ago taken over by Betty Laine, whose Laine Theatre Arts has now a fine large new premises in East Street and a considerable and growing reputation.

o 0 o

Upon retirement I joined the Epsom Probus Club and the Ewell Bowling Club. Why not Ewell for Probus and Epsom for Bowls especially when the Epsom Bowling Club, which was founded in 1909, has for many years had its headquarters by the side of that little footpath next to Ivel Cottage, where I was born, and so close to my present Beech Tree Cottage? It just so happened the one-time Mayor, Fred Paul, asked me to join the former and Bill Loveless, with whom I had already been associated in the Harriers, the Operatic and Nonsuch Opera, asked me to join the latter. The word 'Probus', despite any attempt to find a derivation from Latin or a village in Cornwall, means no more than 'Professional and Business'; a distinction which lingers, recalling my prep. school hiccup. Ewell's bowling green is most pleasantly situated in a peaceful (apart from the occasional clickerty-click from Network South East) corner of the Gibraltar Recreation Ground in West Street, Ewell.

Adjoining is the Epsom and Ewell Football Club's ground. The club, founded there as 'Epsom Town' in 1917, attained a memorable high spot in 1975 when reaching the final of the Football Association Championship Vase at prestigious Wembley.

I am no football fanatic and when some years ago in the Spread Eagle someone pointed out, 'that's Johnny Haynes', it had to be explained to me that the immaculate young man at the next table – a resident of Epsom's Woodcote Park Road – was the brilliant Fulham player who represented England no less than fifty-six times; being Captain on twenty-two occasions.

My brother has since retirement been much involved with the Royal Air Force Benevolent Association and with the Epsom, Ewell and District branch of the Lest We Forget Association.

After the Great War the care of the many disabled ex-service men was somewhat haphazard until the early 1920s. Some inspired initial work by Martha Cunningham prompted, in 1922, the Mayor of Kingston-upon-Thames to call a meeting, at which the Lest We Forget Association was founded with the object 'To keep alive an earnest active interest in the welfare and happiness of disabled men and women, in or out of hospital and homes, who have served or are serving in the Armed Forces'. The Epsom, Ewell and District branch came into being in 1924 with Sir Arthur Glyn as President. Largely under the influence of Stanley Wootton, many local racehorse trainers gave their support. Mrs. Arthur Skilton and Mrs. Tom Walls became devoted workers in the 1930s, with Iris Wall as a long serving Secretary. In a letter dated 1982, which Bob recently lent me, the last mentioned recalls how Lady Sybil Grant initiated the picking of snowdrops (Lord Rosebery's favourite flower) on The Durdans estate for sale for the charity and how the Snowdrop Fund began exactly fifty years earlier. Since the second World War the work of the Association has continued and increased, with many local trades-people and others organising visits, parties, entertainments and transport. The Snowdrop collection in 1987 provided a record £1663. The good work goes on.

It is now some years since I became a member of the Epsom Protection Society. This was founded in 1959 with Brian Fender, Geoffrey Aronson, and subsequently Audrey Cooper, as the prime movers in the conception of an organisation 'to safeguard Epsom's traditional character'. I was happy to be allowed to serve on the committee for a time in the 1980s.

The Society states its objects as follows:

To promote high standards of planning and architecture.
To ensure the preservation, protection, development and improvement of features of historic or public interest.
To ensure that the attractive and leafy residential areas are maintained.
To ensure the preservation and maintenance of the surrounding Green Belt.

To educate the public in the geography, history, natural history and architecture of the area.

An increasing number of people obviously feel, as I do, that the Society's aims are very worth-while so membership continues to grow. There is happily a very good relationship with the Borough Council – a situation that frequently provides useful results.

I have by now mentioned a number of local organisations, and naturally these are the ones with which I have some close relationship or, at least, some special interest. Epsom and Ewell has many social, political, benevolent, religious, sporting and other clubs, but obviously it is not within the scope of this book to catalogue them, neither is it to make a directory of the varied amenities our Borough Council provides.

o 0 o

With others, I expect I have done my share of criticising demolitions, office blocks, traffic schemes and so on, but we undoubtedly have much in Epsom and Ewell for which to be thankful and about which to boast.

It is obviously Epsom Salts and the Derby that have made us famous; but the wonderful situation and great expanse of the Downs, the one time importance of our Spa, the historical connections of The Durdans and other houses, the wide High Street with its tower and the extent of the unspoilt Common are, amongst other things, also notable.

Epsom is now joined to Ewell and all but to Tolworth and Kingston and to Sutton and Wimbledon, yet somehow it still just manages to escape being suburban and not quite part of London. If the proximity to the South London suburbs can be held to be on the debit side, that is more than compensated for on the credit side by the fact that the green country comes right up to within a mile of our town centre. The M25 is close enough to speed our contact with the most distant parts of the country, should we wish. From the top of Ashley Road one can pass through continuous countryside into Sussex or Hampshire without seeing a town or having to travel through any large built-up area. From the north side of the Downs can be viewed the whole of the great metropolis – and its pleasures enjoyed within the hour – yet from the south side one looks across mile after mile of the trees and hills of beautiful Surrey.

If I am not inclined to match the hyperbole of Dickens or the effusiveness of Toland, I hope it may be concluded that I am grateful and still enthusiastic about my native town.

# *Dates*

1618 Traditional date for the discovery of Epsom's Waters.
1629 Reports that the Epsom Well was being much visited.
1663 Visit to the Wells, the Town and The Durdans by Samuel Pepys.
1667 Visit to the Wells, the King's Head, the Downs and the Church by Samuel Pepys.
1672 Thomas Shadwell's play 'Epsom Wells' first produced.
1690s Northey family first in Epsom – Woodcote House.
1707 Livingstone first advertised the New Spa in the town.
1711 John Toland's description of Epsom.
1730s The decline of the Spa.
1756 The present Durdans built.
1779 First running of The Oaks.
1780 First running of The Derby.
1824 Building of the present St. Martin's Parish Church.
1825 Pownall's 'History of Epsom'.
1829 The old Grand Stand built.
1839 First gaslight in the town.
1843 The old Christ Church built.
1847 Epsom's first railway station (In present Upper High Street).
1849 The Literary Society founded.
1849 The Clock Tower built.
1850 Local Health Board established.
1851 Epsom College founded.
1854 The Pond in the middle of the High Street filled in.
1859 Epsom's second railway station (On present site)
1860 C. W. Swete's 'Handbook of Epsom'.
1863 Mrs. Beeton's book of 'Household Management' published.
1870 Epsom Cricket Club founded.
1876 The present Christ Church built.
1878 Lord Rosebery took up residence at The Durdans.
1882 Chuter Ede born.
1883 The Public Hall (later The Palladium) built.
1887 The Cottage Hospital built in Alexandra Road.
1889 Epsom Golf Club founded.
1890 Epsom Harriers founded.
1894 Lord Rosebery became Prime Minister.
1898 The present Post Office in the High Street opened.

1899 First Mental Hospital (The Manor) opened.
1901 Gordon Home's 'Epsom, Its History and Surroundings' published.
1904 James Andrews' 'Reminiscences' published.
1907 St. Martin's Church altered and enlarged.
1909 Epsom Bowling Club founded.
1910 The Cinema Royal and the Electric Cinema opened.
1911 The R.A.C. took over Woodcote Park.
1911 Epsom Operatic Society founded.
1912 Epsom had the first dial telephone exchange in the country.
1913 Suffragette Emily Davison killed at The Derby.
1917 Epsom Town Football Club founded.
1919 Station Sergeant Green killed.
1919 Grand Torchlight Procession to the Downs to celebrate the Peace.
1920 First Epsom to Redhill bus. (later the 406).
1921 First Epsom to Guildford bus. (later the 408).
1922 Epsom Hockey Club founded.
1924 Formation of the Epsom & Ewell Branch of the Lest-We-Forget Association.
1926 Part of a Roman Villa discovered on Epsom/Ashtead Common.
1927 The New Grand Stand completed.
1928 Electrification of the railway completed.
1929 The Capitol Cinema opened.
1929 The Ebbisham Hall opened.
1929 Lord Rosebery died.
1929 The closure of the Epsom Town Station.
1933 The EUDC took over the parishes of Ewell & Cuddington from the ERDC.
1934 Opening of the Town Hall in The Parade.
1937 Epsom & Ewell became a Borough.
1938 The High Street widening programme completed.
1939 Epsom Baths Hall opened in East Street.
1951 Epsom Symphony Orchestra formed.
1957 Demolition of The King's Head.
1959 Nonsuch Palace excavations.
1963 Closure of the Goods Yard in Upper High Street.
1967 Demolition of Pitt Place.
1968 Nonsuch Opera Society formed.
1984 HM the Queen opened the Ashley Centre.
1984 The Epsom Playhouse opened.
1991 Part of the west end of the High Street pedestrianised.
1992 The new Town Hall extension completed.
1992 New Queen's Stand on the Downs opened.
1992 Inaugaration of Evening Race Meetings.
1993 New Market Place completed.
1996 Epsom and Ewell twinned with Chantilly.

**CHAIRMEN OF THE LOCAL BOARD OF HEALTH**

| | |
|---|---|
| Sir Richard Digby Heave Bart | 1850–1853 |
| Jacob George Cope | 1853–1855 |
| Henry Dorling | 1855–1871 |
| William Trotter | 1871–1872 |
| Frederick Lock | 1872–1874 |
| George Ratcliffe Keeling | 1874–1886 |
| James Andrews | 1886–1891 |
| Edwin Burberry Jay | 1891–1895 |

**CHAIRMEN OF THE EPSOM URBAN DISTRICT COUNCIL**

| | |
|---|---|
| Henry Mayson Dorling | 1895–1899 |
| Alfred Withall Aston | 1900–1901 |
| Walter Gerald Langlands | 1902–1903 |
| Frederick William Ledger | 1904–1905 |
| Walter Gerald Langlands | 1906–1907 |
| John Templeton | 1908 |
| George James Beams | 1909–1910 |
| Henry William Saunders | 1911–1912 |
| John Hatchard Smith | 1913 |
| Charles Cropley | 1914–1915 |
| James Weir Gow | 1916–1917 |
| Henry Banks Longley | 1918–1919 |
| James Chuter Ede | 1920–1921 |
| Capt. Thomas B. Johns | 1922–1923 |
| Arthur Moore | 1924–1925 |
| Sidney Smith | 1926–1927 |
| Charles George Irish | 1928–1929 |
| George Edwin Alway | 1930–1931 |
| Harry Skelton | 1932–1933 |
| Herbert William Cushine | 1934 |
| John Wallace | 1935 |
| Claude Edward Gill | 1936 |
| John Samuel Underhill | 1937 |

**MAYORS OF THE BOROUGH OF EPSOM AND EWELL**

| | |
|---|---|
| 1937 | James Chuter Ede. The Charter Mayor. |
| 1937 | Charles Joseph Shaw |
| 1938 | Herbert William Cushine |
| 1939 | George Wills Taylor |
| 1940 | Charles Joseph Shaw |
| 1941 | Walter Charles Littlejohns |
| 1942 | Alfred Charles Marshall |
| 1943 | Jack Alfred Larby |
| 1944 | Albert William Nicholls |
| 1945 | David Reed |
| 1946 | George Edwin Alway |

| | |
|---|---|
| 1947–48 | Thomas William Lewis |
| 1949 | Frank Tomlin |
| 1950 | George Charles Adrian Mann |
| 1951 | Annie Winter |
| 1952 | Charles Robert Bunyan |
| 1953 | Harley Verneau Usill |
| 1954 | Owen Henry Newton Langston |
| 1955 | Ronald Langley Mitchell |
| 1956 | William John Clark |
| 1957 | Albert Willoughby Gardner |
| 1958 | Frank Percival Lobb |
| 1959 | Albert Willoughby Gardner |
| 1959 | Cecil George Harvey |
| 1960 | Frank Hermann Knight |
| 1961 | Phil Aubrey Leslie Hodges |
| 1962 | Richard Barnard Hodgson |
| 1963 | William Alfred Glover |
| 1964 | Laura Mary Woodcock |
| 1965 | Frank Leslie Woolcott |
| 1966 | Hubert William Davison |
| 1967 | John Arthur George Webb |
| 1968 | Thomas George Holland |
| 1969 | Frederick Noel Kirkwood Paul |
| 1970 | Jacob Albert Hutter |
| 1971 | Diana Joyce Fender |
| 1972 | Harold Rhead Newton |
| 1973 | Reginald Eric Gouldthorpe |
| 1974 | William John Clark |
| 1974 | Reginald Arthur Saviel |
| 1975 | Herbert William Chard |
| 1976 | Victor Richard Barrett |
| 1977 | St. John Hewitt Heather |
| 1978 | Leonard Frederick Charles Miller |
| 1979 | Leslie Francis Wood |
| 1980 | Daphne Malcia Harrison |
| 1981 | Michael Newstead Arthur |
| 1982 | William Raymond Carpenter |
| 1983 | Ronald Stanley Gee |
| 1984 | Norma Gillian Fryer |
| 1985 | Emilie Madeleine Fitch Catmur |
| 1986 | Albert Edwin Faulks |
| 1987 | Clifford Marvyn Donald Shearly |
| 1988 | Joyce Mary Storer |
| 1989 | Pamela Myrtle Ballard |
| 1990 | Robert Leonard Lewis |
| 1991 | Brian John Robert Kibble |
| 1992 | Michael John Charlton Staples |

| | |
|---|---|
| 1993 | Herbert Howard Upton |
| 1994 | Derek Robert Hughes |
| 1995 | Charles Edwin Cyril Frazer |
| 1996 | Hazel Ann Dodd |

**TOWN CLERKS**

| | |
|---|---|
| 1937 | Philip Edward Whiteock-Cooper |
| 1945 | Edward Moore |
| 1973 | Douglas Royle Grimes |

**TOWN CLERKS AND CHIEF EXECUTIVES**

| | |
|---|---|
| 1974 | Douglas Royle Grimes |
| 1986 | David John Smith |

**ST. MARTIN'S PARISH CHURCH, EPSOM.**
**VICARS SINCE 1924**

| | |
|---|---|
| Clive Robertson Pattison Muir | 1924–1938 |
| Hugh Compton Warner | 1938–1950 |
| William Guy Howard | 1950–1963 |
| William Henry Purcell | 1963–1969 |
| Frederick Walter Crooks | 1969–1974 |
| Austen Geoffrey Schrives | 1974–1985 |
| Peter John Lloyd | 1985–1992 |
| David Alan Smethurst | 1993 |

**MEMBERS OF PARLIAMENT FOR THE CONSTITUENCY OF EPSOM DURING THE 20TH CENTURY**

| | |
|---|---|
| WILLIAM KESWICK | 1899–1912 |
| HENRY KESWICK | 1912–1918 |
| GEORGE ROWLAND BLADES (Sir George Rowland Blades Bart., and Baron Ebbisham) | 1918–1928 |
| ARCHIBALD RICHARD JAMES SOUTHBY (Sir Archibald Richard James Southby Bart., R.N.) | 1928–1947 |
| MALCOLM STEWART McCORQUODALE (The Right Honourable and Baron McCorquodale of Newton) | 1947–1955 |
| PETER ANTHONY GRAYSON RAWLINSON (Sir Peter Rawlinson, Baron Rawlinson of Ewell) | 1955–1978 |
| ARCHIE GAVIN HAMILTON (The Right Honourable) | 1978 |

# *Family Tree*

**RALPH FURNISS**
Rayffe ffurnisse. Ewell in 1585

|

**RICHARD 1621**
Also 2 sons/3 daughters from 1610–1624

|

**JOHN 1660**
Of Ewell.

|

**JOHN 1684–1754**
From Ewell to Epsom. The Common Fields by the High Street. 1716.
Carpenter. Constable of Epsom 1719
Also 3 sons from 1682–1699

|

**WILLIAM 1739–1776**
Coachman of Epsom.
Also Benjamin 1725–1798. Tailor. Next to The King's Head.
Also 3 sons/3 daughters.

|

**THOMAS 1773–1847**
Tailor. At the Yew Tree Cottages from 1801.
Also 1 son/3 daughters.

|

**WILLIAM THOMAS 1802–1874**
Tailor. Yew Tree Cottage.
Constable of Epsom, Parish Clerk, Collector of Rates.
Also 1 son/3 daughters.

|

**THOMAS 1828–1908**
Founded T. Furniss, Coal Merchants 1870. West Street.
Also James 1833–1898 and George 1837–1899 of G & J Furniss, Builders and Undertakers. 94-100 High Street.
Also 4 sons/2 daughters.

|

**WILLIAM GEORGE 1885–1954**
Coal Merchant. West Street and 100, High Street.
Worple Road, Reigate Road and Cornwall.
Also Thomas 1872, May 1874 and 2 daughters from first marriage.

|

**JOHN 1915 and ROBERT 1920**

# 1992 – 1996

Since first publishing Talk of the Town in 1992 the wide western end of Epsom High Street (partly pedestrianised in 1991) was greatly enhanced by the provision of attractive paving, and a number of trees and seats. The Market Place was completed and officially opened on the twenty fifth of September 1993. It is interesting to note that the right to hold a market on the site was originally given as long ago as 1685 by Charles the Second. A small Information Centre was incorporated into the already restored Clock Tower in 1995.

Another notable change in the High Street was the moving of Lester Bowden's business from No.109 (premises taken over as Waterstone's bookshop) into the historic Spread Eagle building, which had sadly ceased to be an hotel some years before, having been an inn since the late seventeenth century. The indoor market on the one-time Page Motors site was closed down pending development, and the adjacent footpath leading to the railway station was also closed. A further closure, and finally demolition, was that of the Convent of the Sacred Hearts School in Dorking Road, together with the comparatively new convent on the hill behind, part of which then became the proposed site for a new Catholic church to replace that in Heathcote Road.

In the hope of boosting the waining popularity of the Derby, the famous old race was, in 1995, for the first time run on a Saturday instead of the traditional Wednesday, and a number of special events were held in the High Street and in Rosebery Park. At the same time a fine new Paddock was created in front of the 1992 Queen's Stand.

A happy event took place at the Town Hall on the twenty fourth of March 1996, when a ceremony was held to mark the occasion of the twinning of the famous French racing town of Chantilly with Epsom and Ewell. Afterwards the two Mayors attended a celebration at St. Martin's Church. A plaque at the Clock Tower now records the event.

In 1994 the management of the Epsom Playhouse was taken over by Trevor Mitchell. His considerable experience in the professional theatre, coupled with much enthusiasm and energy, soon resulted in improved programmes of a wider range combining professional and community events. There were also some welcome and attractive alterations within the theatre itself. All this was rewarded by a very considerable increase in ticket sales. After Nonsuch Opera's final production in 1993, I concentrated more on presenting illustrated talks, adding a number of musical theatre subjects, and travelling to venues well beyond the Epsom area.

I was particularly pleased when the old Furniss family account and record book of 1728-1836 (described earlier at some length) was found a permanent home at the Victoria and Albert Museum. I had previously written– "There are a lot more Furnisses in San José than Epsom ". In 1993 on our second American trip, Marnie and I had the unusual experience of a barbecue in the hot dusty Costa Rican mountains with a party of twenty six. Everyone present possessed the same name – Furniss. The family tree still begins with 1585. No further significant discoveries concerning former generations have come to light, but it now has the welcome addition of a great grand daughter , Chelsea, in 1993; two grand daughters-in-law, Sarah and Denise, in 1995; and a grand daughter, Lucy, in 1996.

I am happy to say the last three lines in the original edition of Talk of the Town written in 1992 still hold good.